The Bell Witch in Myth and Memory

The
Bell Witch
in Myth and Memory

From Local Legend to International Folktale

RICK GREGORY

The University of Tennessee Press
Knoxville

Library of Congress Cataloging-in-Publication Data
Names: Gregory, Rick S., author.
Title: The Bell witch in myth and memory : from local legend
to international folktale / Rick Gregory.
Description: Knoxville : The University of Tennessee Press, [2023] |
Includes bibliographical references. |
Summary: "While dozens of books and articles
have rehearsed the chilling lore surrounding
the 'infamous Bell Witch of Tennessee,'
Rick Gregory takes a different approach. He illuminates
the oral traditions that preserved and disseminated the tale;
discusses the major factors in its regional, national,
and international spread; analyzes how the legend mirrors
other national and international stories with similar themes; and finally
describes its modern circulation through the World Wide Web
and other technologies. In exploring the Bell Witch story in this manner,
Gregory sheds light not only on the folklore of Tennessee with its strong
tradition of oral history but also provides insight into the persistent,
global phenomenon of folklore itself"—Provided by publisher.
Identifiers: LCCN 2023022312 (print) | LCCN 2023022313 (ebook) |
ISBN 9781621908371 (paperback) | ISBN 9781621908388 (pdf)
Subjects: LCSH: Bell family—Miscellanea. | Poltergeists—Tennessee—
Robertson County. | Folklore—Tennessee—Robertson County.
Classification: LCC BF1473.B37 G74 2023 (print) | LCC BF1473.B37 (ebook)
| DDC 133.1/2976846—dc23/eng/20230624
LC record available at https://lccn.loc.gov/2023022312
LC ebook record available at https://lccn.loc.gov/2023022313

To all those people in Adams, Tennessee;
the rest of the country; and the world who told,
preserved, and passed on the Bell Witch story,
and to those who will do so in the future.

Contents

Illustrations

Preface

Since its inception, the legend of the Bell Witch has been explored and sometimes exploited through various media, including dozens of books and periodicals, thousands of newspaper articles, numerous radio, television, and film productions; and enough podcasts, websites, and documentaries to keep anyone occupied for much of the rest of their life. The Bell Witch, or "Kate," as she is known, has received additional attention in the performing arts as the subject of plays, ballets, a cantata that opened at Carnegie Hall, college lectures, and in songs ranging from country to doom metal. "Old Kate" has even appeared in the pages of *Playboy* magazine. With this fixation in mind, I doubt that the world needs another book about the Bell Witch.

So, why yet another book? Much of what we know (or at least think we know) of the story came from the supernatural aspects of the Bell Witch legend. This book does not focus on the well-known supernatural features of the story—though I do give a summary of the two-hundred-year-old narrative in Chapter 2. My real interest lies in the "bookends" of the tale. As such, this study will explore what people believe, why people believe what they cannot explicitly prove, and why for two hundred years some people have believed, with strong conviction, in the validity of the Bell Witch story.

There is also another question to this familiar folktale: how did the Bell Witch story become known nationwide and, to some degree, worldwide? I began to ask this question after a series of personal experiences. My occupation required that I travel often throughout the United States and Canada. I have worked in several US states and three Canadian provinces.

When people learned I was from Adams in Robertson County, Tennessee, many reacted with some version of: "Oh, the Bell Witch." How did they, so far from the tale's origin, know the Bell Witch story?

In January 2019, I was walking down the beach along the panhandle of Florida and saw a couple walking toward me. We stopped and started a conversation, during which I learned that they were from Sweden and had never been in the United States before this trip. When they found out that I was from Adams, Tennessee, they started talking to each other in Swedish. After a while, the woman looked at me, smiled, and in English said, "the Bell Witch." When asked how they knew about the story, they replied that one of the most popular metal bands in the Nordic countries was a Danish band called Mercyful Fate who had a song called "The Bell Witch." They also liked a Seattle-based doom metal band named Bell Witch. I was intrigued. Before I committed completely to the project, however, I wanted to make sure that the story was prominent in newspapers in the United States, Canada, and elsewhere. I turned to online databases, which uncovered a wealth of information. Thus, I began my quest to uncover how the story had traveled through space and time.

There is one more reason that I decided to write this book. Since I am from Robertson County, dozens of people have asked me about sources that could help them understand various aspects of the Bell Witch legend and how it has survived for two hundred years. Thus, I have provided copious sources to answer these questions.

Before I continue, it is necessary to make four caveats to better understand the purpose of this narrative. First, although I will reference religion, it is not my design to question anyone's religious beliefs. Almost all cultures and societies throughout history have held beliefs in a divine being or beings. While I aim to explore various beliefs, including witches, ghosts, goblins, vampires, zombies, sasquatch/bigfoot/yeti, werewolves, UFOs, Loch Ness Monster, astrology, and so forth, I am not questioning their veracity. I am simply asking, why do people believe what they cannot possibly prove?

Further, it is not my intent to prove or disprove anyone's supernatural beliefs. In my research, I came across an insightful podcast called "encounterscast.com." At the beginning of most episodes, the narrator says, "This podcast covers experiences people have with supernatural entities and paranormal phenomena. We are not interested in proving or disproving experiences of belief." I both endorse and echo this sentiment.

Regarding the title of this work, I borrowed the idea and words from Ralph Waldo Emerson. His poem "Concord Hymn" was used as a hymn at the July 4, 1837, dedication of the Concord, Massachusetts, battle monument commemorating the "first shot" of the Revolutionary War. Similar words were used by writers describing the assassination of Archduke Franz Ferdinand by Gavrilo Princip on June 28, 1914, thus leading to the beginning of World War I. Again, similar words were screamed into a microphone on October 3, 1951, by a baseball announcer in response to Bobby Thomson's walk-off home run. This "shot heard around the world" won the National League pennant for the New York Giants, who defeated the Brooklyn Dodgers. This concept has been used numerous times to describe an important event. Hyperbolic as the symbolism may be, if it is good enough for Emerson, it is good enough for me.

It is also important to note that while I am a historian by training and have written local history books and taught history at the college level, this is not exclusively an academic book. My goal is to reach a midpoint between scholars and a general audience concerning the best-known pieces of folklore in American culture.

Last, I am assuming that most readers will have a working knowledge of the Bell Witch story. If this is not true for you, familiarizing yourself with the legend will foster a deeper understanding of and appreciation for this narrative. An overview of the story can also be found in Chapter 2.

Acknowledgments

I would like to take this opportunity to thank several people for sharing ideas and information with me as I researched and wrote this book. William (Bo) Adams shared his knowledge and books from his private Bell Witch collection, which strengthened this book. Dewey Edwards and Timothy Henson, both published Bell Witch authors, provided insights into the story. Bill Jones, a local Robertson County historian, shared with me many ideas about the Bell Witch. David Alford wrote the play, *Spirit: The Authentic Story of the Bell Witch of Tennessee*. For over two decades, this play has brought thousands of people to Adams, Tennessee to experience the legend. And thanks to Annie Patterson and Donna Heffner, owners of the Alexander-Perrigo House in Historic Rugby, Tennessee. Their many kindnesses made Rugby the perfect place to write this book.

The

Bell Witch

in Myth and Memory

one

THE POWER OF A STORY

If history were written in the form of stories,
it would never be forgotten.

—ATTRIBUTED TO RUDYARD KIPLING

I believe God gave us one final gift . . . he gave us stories.

—WILLIAM KENT KRUEGER,
This Tender Land

No one now likes to own a belief in evil spirits or
witches, but considers it would be a pity to receive
harm from neglecting so easy a precaution
[as hanging up an old horseshoe.]

—GEORGE ROBERTS,
History of Lyme Regis and Charmouth

You've been warned against looking in the mirror
and saying you don't believe in the Bell Witch. You've
heard that if you sneak away with even a pebble from
the Bell Witch cave you'll meet with disaster. People say
the Bell Witch really existed and that she still haunts a
cave in Adams, Tennessee. Tonight, as you crawl into
bed, you decide: Do you believe in the Bell Witch?

—NICOLE GARTON,
"Do you Believe in the Bell Witch,"
Nashville Tennessean, October 22, 2001

The origins of legends can be traced to the spoken word and storytellers. Oral renditions were followed by the written word in newspapers, magazines, journals, and books. As technology developed, information became widely available via radio, television, films, computers, internet, podcasts, blogs, and so on. While these pathways of communication are important, the spoken word and storytelling are dominant means of propagating myths, folklore, and legends. This I have learned through personal experience. I was born and have spent most of my life living in Robertson County, Tennessee, the home of the Bell Witch legend.[1] I descend from many talented storytellers, a skill that has been very useful in my professional life over the past three decades. When I first began public speaking, I heard firsthand many speakers bore the audience through their perfunctory, factual deliveries. I watched the eyes of listeners "glaze over," with some napping and others driven to distraction. I also witnessed, however, speakers who could hold their listeners' attention as long as they spoke.

The difference was in their storytelling. I learned that if I recited facts, the audience might remember them for only a short period of time. If I told them a story, they could remember the story forever. I initially realized this when I spoke at a conference at which I had presented years before. At the event, someone reminded me of a story I had told at a similar conference a decade prior. This happened to me many times. I learned that if I wanted my audience to remember an important fact or point, hide it in a story. Phillip Pullman put it simply, "If you want your listeners to remember what you say, tell them a story."[2]

If this is in fact true, what makes it so? Maybe the need to tell and hear stories is embedded in our collective DNA.[3] This idea was supported by Reynolds Price, who wrote: "A need to tell and hear stories is essential to the species homo sapiens; second in necessity apparently after nourishment and before love and shelter. Millions survive without love or home, almost none in silence; the opposite of silence leads quickly to narrative, and the sound of story is the dominant sound of our lives, from the small accounts or our day's events to the vast incommunicable constructs."[4]

It is also important to remember that some of our familiar narratives today are in fact ancient. As Ferris Jabr wrote, "If certain beloved stories have endured for thousands of years, they tell us something important about narrative itself."[5] In Western culture *The Iliad*, *The Odyssey*, and *The Aeneid* are just three of many stories that began as oral tales before being written down. Almost all cultures have foundational stories that are still told and read today—which provides important context when considering how the Bell Witch legend has lasted for two centuries and shows no sign of being forgotten.

There are several reasons why the legend has lasted and will continue to last. Stories can make a listener feel a range of emotions. The most memorable stories evoke a core emotion or emotions from the listener, including sadness, fear, anger, joy, excitement, and disgust. The recipient of a story usually wants not just to hear, but to be affected by, the story. The Bell Witch legend can stir each of these core emotions during the narrative.[6]

Shared stories can also help individuals fit in with peers and develop an ability to tell their own stories. Storytelling can also help the teller and forge a connection with family, friends, and community. This sense of connection is vital for all of us as we seek to understand ourselves and our role in other peoples' lives and their roles in our own lives.[7] Stories can transcend time and bond generations together—even generations that never knew each other. The Bell Witch legend did just that for generations of people living in Robertson County, Tennessee, the rest of the country, and to some extent, the world.

The major components of storytelling are folklore, myth, legend, and gossip. The Bell Witch story is likely a product of all four, with folklore being the most important. Jane Polley defines folklore as "the body of traditional customs, beliefs, tales, songs . . . that are transmitted by word of mouth from one generation . . . to the next."[8] She included a Bell Witch story entitled "The Bell Witch: An Overseeing Haunt" in her book.[9]

Folklore does not have to be believable to be a good story. Even without suspension of disbelief, these tales are part of the experience of being human and can be entertaining. This is true, even when the stories themselves are not. In addition, folklore can be used in many ways to help people. According to one scholar, it can "promote learning, problem solving, cultural conservation, improve quality of life and enhance identity and a sense of community."[10]

A legend is defined as a subgenre of folklore that may be a mixture of truth and fiction. Legends are usually larger-than-life stories such as Robin Hood, Beowulf, Davy Crockett, Paul Bunyan, and Pecos Bill. A legend can also reveal information about the society and culture that produced it. In their article in the *Journal of American Folklore*, Arthur Palmer Hudson and Pete Kyle McCarter make the case that the Bell Witch story was a folk legend that grew out of rural Tennessee and Mississippi.[11]

Legends and myths have much in common. Both can be used to en-tertain and provide information for storytelling. The key difference is that a myth can be a legend with deep symbolic meaning. Myths can be used to explore a culture's traditions and beliefs to explain supernatural events.[12] Myths can also be used to bind together individuals who share the same physical space and culture into one people. According to Yuval Noah Harari in his book *Sapiens: A Brief History of Human Kind*, belief in common myths made civilization possible. He suggests that, "Any large-scale human cooperative is rooted in common myths."[13] He continues, "Myths and fictions accustomed people, nearly from the moment of birth, to think certain ways, to behave in accordance with certain standards, to want certain things, and observe certain rules."[14]

This concept can be applied to United States history. As with all civiliza-tions, myths have been used in the United States to frame citizens' views of the nation and its history. A modern college US history book concluded, "Historical myths and legends are needful in establishing national identity and stimulating patriotic pride.[15] To relate this information to the Bell Witch story in any meaningful way, it is important to understand that a belief in witches has been part of most civilizations and cultures for as long as humankind itself. It is reasonable then to assume that a belief in witchcraft has been part of the American experience from the beginnings of its settlement.[16]

The last form of storytelling worthy of examination is one that often goes overlooked—gossip. Briefly put, to gossip is to discuss someone or something that is not present. Gossip can be malicious, educational, a means of bonding, or simply a way to pass the time. Regardless of its in-tent, gossip has been part of the human experience since the invention of language. In *Sapiens*, Harari agrees with this assertion and even goes a step further by suggesting that a desire to gossip might be a reason for the development of language itself.[17]

It is easy to imagine that farm families close to the Bell homeplace during the events from 1817 to 1820 and afterward would gossip about what was taking place at the Bell farm. It was such gossiping that helped form the storytelling, myths, and legends that developed the Bell Witch story that we know today. The continuity of this gossiping is evidenced by the number of books, articles, novels, plays, podcasts, and so on, that have been produced in this millennia.

Not to be overlooked, the roles ethnicity and geography play in the Bell

Witch story are worthy of examination and analysis. It is no coincidence that this tale originated in the upper South, as many of the people who came to Tennessee migrated from North Carolina and Virginia and were direct descendants of immigrants from England, Scotland, and Ireland. As they traveled westward across an ocean and by land to middle Tennessee and Kentucky, each generation brought its folklore, legends, myths, gossips, and beliefs.

The South is noted for its folklore, stories, and storytelling, especially concerning supernatural events. In *A Treasury of Southern Folklore: Stories, Ballads, Traditions, and Folkways of the People of the South*, B. H. Botkin refers to the South as a "storied region." He also quotes Irvin S. Cobb as follows: "It is a fancy of mine—although a fancy based on a considerable amount of firsthand observation—that there is a storytelling belt in this country, it starts at the high-water mark on the shores of Eastern Virginia and it stretches westward through Tennessee and Kentucky, broadening out to include southern Indiana and parts of North Carolina. "[18] More recently, the University of North Carolina Press published a volume entitled *The New Encyclopedia of Southern Culture, Vol. 14: Folklife*, which supported this view.[19]

The Bell Witch legend has been recognized as one of the best Southern ghost stories. An article in a Middle Tennessee newspaper proclaimed that "The South is alive with stories of ghosts and the Bell Witch story is one of the best known."[20] In the same vein, Floyd E. Randall published a book on Southern mysteries and included the Bell Witch story as one of his entries.[21] Even more recently, prominent writer Rick Bragg wrote, "Being a Southern writer, I usually stayed in a place with some history which (down here) means it's haunted."[22]

Although the link between the Bell Witch story and the South is strong, the link between the tale and North Carolina is stronger. Robertson County was part of North Carolina's military district after the Revolutionary War, with the state having given land grants to its soldiers after the war. Incidentally, many people who settled in the county were from North Carolina. The Bell family, no exception to this trend, migrated from North Carolina to what became Robertson County after Tennessee obtained statehood in 1796.

It stands to reason that new settlers in Middle Tennessee brought their beliefs and superstitions with them. In *The Spirit of the Mountains*, Emma B. Miles retells the North Carolina story of Old Nance, a poltergeist who haunted the Beaver family in the western part of the state. She could be heard but not seen. Old Nance especially targeted Bill, the father of the Beaver family, for abuse. She referred to him as "Old Leatherhead." When he asked her on several occasions why she hated him, she would give him different answers. One answer was, "You plowed up my bones once." Another retort was "You know you're the meanest man that ever broke the world's bread." She predicted that she would kill the Beaver father. She said she would follow him to the end of the world." When he died in his bed, people said that he was killed by witchcraft.

Despite her dislike of Mr. Beaver, Old Nance was especially kind to Sairy, Mrs. Beaver. When Sairy "was taken down rael sick," Old Nance kept the flies off her. She also provided the sick woman with strawberries, even though they were out of season. On another occasion, a drunk man came to the Beaver house and was disrespectful to Sairy. Old Nance "slapped him good" and led him of out the house "by the nose."

When it came to other people, she could alternate between good and bad. Often, she had a screeching, intolerable voice, and at other times could sit and have a cordial conversation with family members and guests. She would visit local churches, discuss scriptures, and called a local preacher "Old Sugarmouth." She often pulled the covers off a sleeping person in the middle of the night. [23] The purpose of this rendition of the "Old Nance" story was to draw links between it and the Bell Witch story. There are similar versions of each tale in the Bell Witch legend. *The Spirit of the Mountains* was published in 1905, over a century after the Bell Witch event. We don't know if early North Carolina settlers brought the "Old Nance" stories with them to Middle Tennessee or if it was borrowed, in part, from the Bell Witch folklore. Either way, the story was told in both places. Folklorist B. A. Botkin recorded that the Bell Witch story was the best in its class and that the Beaver family was a parallel to the Bell family story.[24]

Kentucky folktales often reflect themes similar to Tennessee tales, which is relevant to understanding the Bell Witch stories because the Red River community, where the Bell family lived, was just a few miles from the Kentucky border. William Lynwood Montell, author of *Tales of Kentucky Ghosts*, was a folk studies professor at Western Kentucky University in Bowling Green who collected and published several books on supernatural stories in the state. Some had commonalities with the Bell Witch legend.[25]

As in the case with North Carolina, Kentucky, and the South, Tennessee is noted for its folklore and folktales. According to *Tennessee: A Guide to the State*, a 1939 book by the Work Projects Administration, Tennessee is known for "taking its folkish pattern from habits, beliefs, and forms rooted in the remote past of the British Isles . . . [and] . . . the folkways of Tennessee are part of the general regional culture of the South."[26] In 1940, an article in a Tennessee newspaper suggested that "Tennesseans need not go to foreign climates for story material. The state holds a wealth of native folklore."[27]

The best-known folklore story in the state was undoubtedly the Bell Witch. Local Montgomery County, Tennessee, historian Ursula Beach, wrote, "The greatest contributions to local folklore were volumes dealing with the Bell Witch."[28] This idea was supported by a Clarksville (TN) *Leaf-Chronicle* newspaper article in 1989 that declared "The Bell Witch Legend Lives on in Folklore of Tennessee."[29] Decades earlier, another newspaper writer foreshadowed the previous article when she wrote that "Ghosts walk in many Tennessee homes."[30]

Throughout this chapter, we have meandered through Scotland, England, Ireland, North Carolina, Kentucky, and Tennessee, so that we could reach our destination at the Bell farm in Robertson County, Tennessee. While on this journey, we have explored the many aspects of storytelling. Without this information, we cannot understand how the Bell Witch story became known nationwide and, in some aspects, worldwide.

Imagine a family thousands of years ago sitting around a fire in a cave. The oldest male is telling the story about a successful hunt he undertook when he was young. Because language was in the early stage of development, he uses a spare amount of words along with grunts and gestures to illustrate the story. This story will become part of the folklore of his descendants.[31]

Bell Witch stories also appeared in Mississippi and Alabama. Some Bell family members moved to these two states after John Bell's death. The stories followed the migrants and add new Bell Witch legends in both states.

Again, imagine yourself in a world before electricity, television, radio, computers, and the internet. People told each other stories to entertain, pass along history, teach values, develop communication skills, develop a sense of family and community, and bring meaning and beauty to dull lives. Sitting around the fireplace at night, lounging on the front porch on hot August days, gathered around a potbellied stove at the local general store, eating at a church dinner on the ground, loafing and whittling in front of the courthouse, and in dozens of other social occasions, Robertson Countians told and retold the Bell Witch tales and other stories. And, being human, they gossiped about the events on the Bell farm. In the telling, each generation passed the folklore to their children and grandchildren, who would continue the process.

Donald Davidson, Fugitive poet at Vanderbilt University during the 1930s, contributor to the book *I'll Take My Stand,* and a longtime English professor at the university, began his teaching career in Robertson County. He recalled, "My first teaching job, in 1910, took me into the locality where the Bell Witch first flourished. I taught at Cedar Hill, which is a few miles north of Springfield . . . When I taught at Cedar Hill, I knew people who were kin to the Bells, and I also knew some who (as I recall) were old enough to have talked with "survivors"—so to speak—of the Bell Witch affair. I heard the story of the Bell Witch many times.[32] And the story continued to grow.

Through the years, decades, and two centuries, people heard, watched, and read the stories of the Bell Witch. Some people heard this popular tale and thought of it as nothing more than an entertaining yarn. Others heard the story and believed it, in whole or in part. Why did some people believe this story, even though it could not be proven? Moreover, what other stories did people believe that still cannot be proven and why did they believe them? A thorough examination of these questions will be discussed in a subsequent chapter.

Richard Russo has written many novels, short stories, and screenplays. When thinking about the process of writing, he simply concludes, "We tell stories because we must."[33] Perhaps the author must tell, but the reader has choices. And, when readers consume, the author has the distinct opportunity to influence them in not only what to believe, but also *why* they should believe it. This authority is significant because, from the beginning of recorded time, humans have demonstrated a capacity for superstition and have shown a proclivity to believe strange things, hoaxes, and other stories that they cannot prove to be true.[34]

Recent surveys of paranormal beliefs support the view that many Americans believe in some paranormal events. One poll asked about belief in seven major supernatural events. Three-quarters of participants believed in at least one of the paranormal items. Thus, only "one fourth of Americans surveyed did not hold any of the seven beliefs." Over half of those surveyed believed that physical locations could be haunted by spirits.[35] What exactly do people believe in for which no irrefutable evidence exists? The following paragraphs will explore several of these beliefs at greater length. It is important to note that this discussion is only a small sampling, and therefore not representative of all existing paranormal or fringe beliefs, and some of the examples concern historical characters and events.

THE JERSEY DEVIL

The Jersey Devil is a witch-based legend that predates the Bell Witch story by nearly a century. According to the story, in 1735, a witch named Mother Leeds gave birth to a monster with the shape of a malformed horse and piercing red eyes. The beast escaped through the chimney of the house and disappeared into the Pine Barrens of New Jersey. From this hideout, the Jersey Devil terrorized generations of locals and visitors alike. In a recent book, Brian Regal and Frank J. Esposito explore how this story grew and survived as well as the political, cultural, and religious roots of its creation.[36]

GEORGE WASHINGTON COULD NOT TELL A LIE

George Washington's virtue has been both extolled and mythologized. The oral tradition surrounding our first president remains strong today, and one of the frequently recounted stories regarding Washington's character concerns a cherry tree. As the story goes, the young Washington was asked by his father if he had chopped down a prized cherry tree on the family farm. The young future president answered, "Father, I cannot tell a lie, yes, I chopped down the cherry tree." This story, written only one year after Washington's death, was passed down by generations of Americans as proof of Washington's unwavering truthfulness. The story, however, was not true. It was invented by Mason (Parson) Weems in an early biography of the country's first president. It was Weems's desire to present Washington as a perfect role model and to provide moral instruction for America's youth.

In her recent biography of Washington, Alexis Coe begins with a list of ten things that she calls "Lies We Believe About the Man Who Could Not Tell Them." Despite his reputation for stringent honestly, Washington repeatedly lied to the British during the Revolutionary War.

He also did not have wooden teeth, nor did he kneel to pray at Valley Forge, nor skip a silver dollar across the Potomac River. These are just a few of the Washington stories that are either false or embellished—but people have believed them nonetheless.[37]

PRESIDENTIAL CURSE

Another belief about our chief executives that cannot be substantiated is the "presidential curse." As the legend has it, during the War of 1812, Shawnee leader Tecumseh and his fighters sided with Great Britain against the Americans. At the Battle of the Thames in Ontario, Canada, General William Henry Harrison won a decisive victory over Tecumseh's army and the Native American leader was fatally wounded in the battle. Before he died, Tecumseh placed a curse on Harrison and the American presidency. The prophesy was that Harrison would become president and die in office and that every twenty years another president would die in office. In another version of the story Tecumseh's brother, Tenskwatawa, delivered the curse. This popular fabrication most likely originated in an article published in a 1931 edition of *Ripley's Believe It or Not.*[38] Even today, there are still believers. Interest in the curse resurfaces every twenty years. Unsurprisingly, the 2020 election year was no exception.[39]

THE GREAT MOON HOAX OF 1835

On August 21, 1835, the *New York Sun* published the first of six articles about the discovery of life and civilization on the moon. The author of the hoax was a fictitious character named "Dr. Andrew Grant." The articles, which were reprinted in other newspapers, claimed that the invention of a "revolutionary" telescope made these discoveries possible. Among the amazing findings were bat-like, winged humanoids who built temples as well as numerous animals, including unicorns, that lived among trees, oceans, and beaches.[40]

BIGFOOT, SASQUATCH, YETI, SKUNK APE, ETC.

This legend has endured in the United States and Canada since the early 1800s and centers around humanlike creatures that might be missing links between homosapiens and apelike creatures. They were hairy, walked upright, and avoided human contact. Even given their propensity for solitude, people in North America claim to have seen these reclusive creatures and, on occasion, have even photographed them. In the Pacific Northwest, they are usually called Bigfoot or Sasquatch.

In the Himalayas, Siberia, and Central and East Asia, these creatures are referred to as Yetis or Abominable Snowmen. Along the Gulf Coast and the Southern Atlantic coast, a comparable creature is called the Skunk Ape and other similar names.[41]

Prior to European settlement, Seminole myths told stories of apelike characters that have persisted into the present. A recent *Smithsonian* magazine article explored why so many still want to believe in Bigfoot. Their study suggested that people specifically want to believe in things that they cannot prove are true. The legend of Bigfoot captured the imaginations of generations of people around the world and became a pop culture icon. As is the case of the Bell Witch, this legend has spawned books, articles, websites, television shows, and films. Two of the more popular movies were *Harry and the Hendersons* (1987) and *The Man Who Killed Hitler and Then the Bigfoot* (2018). In an effort to raise money by taking advantage of human gullibility, an elected official in Oklahoma recently proposed creating "a bigfoot hunting season as a 'revenue creator,' complete with permits, fees, and a $25,000 reward for anyone who manages to trap a live bigfoot."[42]

THE CARR'S CREEK CRITTER

Bigfoot and similar creatures do not, however, exemplify this entire folktale genre. Numerous other tales in North America tell of sightings of beasts comprised of body parts from more than one animal. Examples include pukwundgies, jackalopes, and El Chupacabras.

Additionally, many small rural areas have stories about spotting strange, never-before-seen animals that prey on livestock. One example occurred in Robertson County, Tennessee, the same county that produced the Bell Witch folklore. The following are a series of articles that appeared in the *Robertson County Times* in 1966: June 16, "Leaping Lena! A Hyena?"; June 23, "Critter From Carr's Creek Elusive, Hogs, Dogs, Afraid of Unseen Prowler"; June 30, "Farmer Hears Howl; Carr's Creek Critter on the Prowl"; July 7, "Would be 'Critter' Hunters Ire Farmers; Worry Officers";

July 14, "Search For the 'Critter' Goes Airbourne"; July 24, "Mother Nature 'Grounds' Helicopter Search for Critter"; July 28, "Elusive Critter Still at Large: Remain of Calf"; September 1, "Critter Might Be a Coyote"; September 29, "Should County Folks Have Cried Wolf."

The whole "episode" appeared in the newspaper for a little over three months. Even so, the story of the so-called Carr's Creek Critter lives in the memories of many Robertson Countians, even those who were not alive in 1966. Storytelling is a powerful form of communication.[43] In addition, a novel based on the Carr's Creek Critter was published in 2020.[44]

THE MOTHMAN

The folklore story of the Mothman began in Point Pleasant, West Virginia. Over time, the tale became entwined with another local legend from the late 1700s to the early 1800s, the tale of Shawnee Chief Cornstalk. According to the story, Cornstalk and some of his followers were lured into Fort Randolph, near present-day Point Pleasant, to attend a peace conference in November 1777. Cornstalk and most of his followers were killed by white soldiers. Before he died, Cornstalk put a curse on the area.

Predictably, most of the negative events that happened in the area were blamed on the curse. The most disastrous of these events was the collapse of the Silver Bridge, which spanned the Ohio River connecting Point Pleasant and Southern Ohio. On December 15, 1967, forty-six people died and many more were injured. During the same period, an explosion at the town jail that killed five people was also blamed on Cornstalk's curse.

Another account from the 1960s became entwined with the curse and the collapse of the bridge. The November 12, 1966, issue of the *Point Pleasant Register* newspaper carried the following article: "Couples See Man-Sized Bird . . . Creature . . . Something." For the next year, there were reports of sightings of what became known as the Mothman. One of the storylines was that the Mothman came to Point Pleasant to try to warn local citizens about the future collapse of the Silver Bridge. The story of the Mothman soon traveled from the *Point Pleasant Register* and local citizens to newspapers and people around the country. A book titled *The Mothman Prophecies* was published in 1975. In 2002, a film by the same name, starring Richard Gere, was viewed on movie screens nationwide. In further proof of the popularity of this legend, every year Point Pleasant holds a Mothman festival.[45]

THE LOCH NESS MONSTER

One of Europe's best-known folklore creatures, and one that has developed a worldwide following, is Scotland's Loch Ness Monster. Loch Ness is the largest freshwater body in the United Kingdom and is the focal point of a long history of lore concerning water-based monsters. Among them are the boobrie, buarachbhgoi, biasd na srogaig, waterbulls, and water horses.

In the 1930s, the Loch Ness Monster eclipsed all of these cryptids in Scottish mythology. In 1933, Aldie and John Mackay spotted something large that they did not recognize in the water along the shore of Loch Ness. There was a long tradition in the area of belief in the existence of a large, long-necked prehistoric looking creature in Loch Ness. The Mackays told a friend of theirs who happened to be a newspaper reporter about the sighting. He wrote about the incident in the *Inverness Courier,* provoking a response by those who read the story and remembered the folklore. As more reports of creature sightings emerged, the Loch Ness Monster story was born, and spread by the press throughout Europe and the rest of the world. The monster became so popular, it was given a colloquial name: Nessie. Through the decades, scientists and other interested amateur sleuths attempted to find the creature. Several pictures supposedly of the Loch Ness Monster have been made public. Although there is no verifiable proof, the Loch Ness Monster still lives in the imagination of its believers.[46]

ASTROLOGY

As long as there has been sapiens on Earth, they have looked at the sky with awe and fascination. This interest contributed to the birth of astrology. Astrology is the belief that a person's life, character, and destiny are controlled, at least in part, by the pattern of the sky at the moment of birth. In *The Fated Sky*, Benson Bobrick wrote, "Such an idea is as old as the world is old—that all things bear the imprint of the moment they are born."[47]

Western astrology began in Mesopotamia and spread throughout the Western world. People use the stars and planets to make life decisions and understand their fates. Theodore Roosevelt, Charles de Gaulle, and Ronald Reagan were three of many powerful people who consulted astrology for guidance. In my youth, as a boy born in Robertson County, I knew people who consulted *Farmer's Almanac* to help them decide when to plant tobacco and other crops. New belief in astrology has had a rebirth in the last few years. A 2017 Pew Report concluded that almost 30 percent of Americans are believers. Some researchers suggest the number may be higher. Furthermore, a large percentage of Americans check their horoscope daily. [48]

UFOS

In a similar vein, a considerable number of Americans believe in unidentified flying objects, another belief dating back thousands of years. The best-known recent event that reenergized the debate about UFOs happened in Roswell, New Mexico, in the summer of 1947. A New Mexico rancher found debris in his sheep pasture. Officials from the nearby military base reported that the wreckage came from a crashed weather balloon. Thus began a debate about UFOs that continues today. An example of this debate can be found in two recent articles: *The Week* magazine's "Why the Military Isn't Scoffing Anymore" and Faye Flam's piece in *The Skeptical Inquirer*, "What We Get Wrong When We Talk about UFOs."[49]

Since Roswell, the surge of interest in UFOs has generated a wealth of articles, books, television shows, websites, and podcasts. Even so, many Americans probably found a renewed interest because of films. Dozens of big screen movies about UFOs have been produced in the decades since Roswell; three of the best known are *The Day the Earth Stood Still* (1951, 2008), *Close Encounters of the Third Kind* (1977), and *ET* (1982).

At least one of the many UFO internet sites found a link between unidentified flying objects and the Bell Witch. The May 1, 2019, issue of *UFO Digest* features a post by Sean Casteel, who draws a connection. Casteel also co-authored a book about supernatural events, including the Bell Witch Story.[50]

THE LITTLE GREEN MEN OF KELLY, KENTUCKY

Kelly, the site of the "little green men story," is forty miles north of Adams, home of the Bell Witch. The town is in Christian County, Kentucky, and Hopkinsville is the county seat. On August 21, 1955, five adults and seven children arrived at the police station in Hopkinsville to tell their story about a spaceship landing close to their house with "little green men" exiting it. The little green men laid siege to their house, but they fought the aliens off with guns long enough to escape to Hopkinsville.

Local law enforcement officials and representatives from Fort Campbell, a local military base, investigated the claims. No proof was found. Even so, newspaper articles spread the story throughout the region and the country. I live in Adams, a short distance from Kelly, and have been told by several people in the area that they believe the little green men story. Some residents have also told me that they knew someone who saw the space visitors.[51]

GHOSTS/POLTERGEISTS

In German, poltergeist means "noisy ghost." I will use the terms "poltergeist" and "ghost" interchangeably. Belief in ghosts is as old as civilization in almost all cultures. Often spirits are reported as benign, but some are seen as harmful. In their most gentle state, they make noises, move objects, appear out of nowhere, and on occasion, communicate with humans. In their more violent appearances, they hurt people; in the story of the Bell Witch, they kill. One of the best-known visitations was known as the "Epworth Ghost," which supposedly haunted John Wesley's family in England. Wesley was the most influential founder of the Methodist Church. There will be more about Wesley later in this chapter.[52]

WITCHCRAFT

As is the case with ghosts, belief in witches is as old as history. European history, especially during the Middle Ages, was noted for violence against women accused of being witches. Much of this negative view of witches came from Old Testament pronouncements against the craft.[53] Europeans brought their prejudices and violence toward women believed to have supernatural powers with them to the Americas.[54]

The most infamous example of mass hysteria over witchcraft in Colonial America took place in 1692–1693 in Salem, Massachusetts. Of the over two hundred women and men accused of witchcraft, thirty were found guilty and nineteen were executed by hanging. Of those executed, fourteen were women and five were men.[55] It is important to note that, as proven in part by the Salem Witch trials, men could be witches too.

Further, as proven by the Bell Witch story, belief in witches was not confined to New England in the 1600s. Additionally, a positive view of witchcraft has survived to the present and is seeing resurgent popularity.[56]

WEREWOLVES

Werewolf is Old English for "man-wolf." Legends of werewolves can be found throughout Europe, Asia, the Americas, and other areas. One of the best-known versions of this legend in the United States is called the "Bray Road Beast," sometimes the "Wisconsin Werewolf." The creature has been described as a cross between a six-to-seven-foot man covered in fur with the head of a wolf or a bear. Sightings have been reported since the 1930s. Many of the reports resemble the Carr's Creek Critter story in Robertson County, Tennessee.

Of course, it goes without saying that the beliefs outlined above cannot be explicitly proven to be true. While a lack of proof does not necessarily make an idea false, belief without proof is open to question. I personally know people in Oregon who claim they saw Bigfoot and others who swear they saw the Carr's Creek Critter in Robertson County, Tennessee. Furthermore, I have connections to people through mutual friends who attest that they saw the little green men of Kentucky. Since I did not see these things myself, I can question the veracity of their accounts.

I also have several acquaintances who strongly believe that they have seen flying saucers and space aliens. Though I have not seen any extraterrestrial phenomena myself, I believe it is logical and rational that we are not alone in the universe. Though I cannot prove it and have never witnessed it, I believe it anyway. This raises the question: why do people, including me, believe what they cannot prove? The rest of this chapter will explore this question.

This list will not be exhaustive, and we could reasonably include conspiracies when discussing subjects people believe in without evidence: for example, the earth is flat; the 1969 moon landing was staged in the Arizona desert; the COVID-19 virus is a hoax; the Holocaust did not happen; the pyramids were built by aliens; vampires, werewolves, and zombies exist, and so on. Some people also superstitiously believe that the following bring good luck: horseshoes, four-leaf clovers, being a "beginner," finding a penny heads-up, knocking on wood, making a wish on a wishbone, itchy palms, tossing spilled salt over your shoulder, and more. The following are believed to bring bad luck: a black cat crossing your path, the number 13, walking under a ladder, breaking a mirror, Friday the 13th, opening an umbrella inside a house, and so on.

These conspiracies and superstitions compel us to question why people are eager to believe in things they cannot prove. Perhaps they do not even know why they believe in these phenomena. While we cannot discuss all beliefs that strain credulity, it is safe to say that most of us believe in something we cannot prove. There are several reasons why. Some concepts to be explored in these pages are generalized in order to demonstrate a connection between folklore and the psyche; other concepts will relate directly to the Bell Witch legend.[57]

IT JUST MAKES SENSE

Earlier, I referenced my convictions that we are not alone in the universe—despite my inability to completely justify this belief. I further suggested that belief without evidence is virtually universal, which is true of even some of the greatest minds on the planet. In 2006, John Brockman edited a book that put forth this challenge to over one hundred scientists and other thinkers, asking, "Great minds can sometimes guess the truth before they have either the evidence or arguments for it. What do you believe is true, even though you cannot prove it?[58] One of the thinkers, Mihaly Csikszentmihalyi, answered this way: "I can prove almost nothing I believe in. I believe the earth is round but I cannot prove it, nor can I prove the earth revolves around the sun . . . all of these and millions of other beliefs are based on faith in a community of knowledge whose proofs I am willing to accept, hoping they will accept on faith a few measly claims to proof I might advance."[59] If more than one hundred of the smartest people on the planet believe what they cannot prove without reproach, then we all can.

I WAS TOLD BY A CREDIBLE SOURCE

One of the best-known cases of a ghost/poltergeist haunting, the Epworth Ghost, took place in England in 1716–1717. The experience happened in the childhood home of John Wesley, one of the most prominent founders of the Methodist Church. Wesley's father preached at the Epworth church and the family lived in the rectory. Although John Wesley did not see or hear the ghost himself, he saw and heard other people, including his parents, describe the haunting. Wesley often referred to the events of the haunting as definitively true. He also spoke and wrote about his belief that witches and witchcraft were at work in the world.[60] Several writers have found links between the Epworth Ghost and the Bell Witch. Gladys Barr wrote books about each of the apparitions for the Famous Witches Series. Harriet Miller, who wrote *The Bell Witch of Middle Tennessee*, also saw similarities with the Epworth Ghost.[61]

Newspaper articles called additional attention to the commonalities between the two supernatural experiences. In 1940, the Guntersville (AL) *Advertiser-Gleam* published a series of articles by William Nabors called "True Ghost Stories." In one of his pieces, Nabors suggests that "The Famous Bell Witch of Robertson County, Tennessee is somewhat parallel with the Wesley ghost." In a 1972 article in the *Nashville Tennessean* entitled "Bell Witch Broke Her Date," Floy Beatty also draws a connection between the Bell Witch and the Epworth Ghost. In all these publications, strange noises, especially knocking sounds as well as items moving "as if by an invisible hand" occurred. In each case, religious leaders ascribed the strange events to malevolent supernatural forces.[62] If Wesley himself, the founder of the Methodist Church, believed in witchcraft and "malevolent forces," it stands to reason that when strange events occurred at the Bell homestead in 1817 locals were eager to attribute the happenings to the supernatural. After all, Methodism was one of the fastest-growing denominations in Middle Tennessee in the early 1800s.

The story of the Epworth Ghost exemplifies how belief can be spread by word of mouth. This is also true regionally. Dewey Edwards, a writer who lives only a few miles from Adams, Tennessee, has written extensively about supernatural experiences in the area. In his book *Ghostly Whispers*, he proclaims, "The events published herein are all true, real life encounters with the paranormal, as experienced by me and/or members of my family spanning a period of several years."[63] Edwards is certainly not alone in his beliefs in paranormal occurrences.

WITCHCRAFT IN THE BIBLE

A 2006 Baylor Institute for Studies of Religion found that 27.4 percent of Americans have paranormal beliefs. The same study reported that 23 percent of Southerners believe that they have lived in or visited a house that is haunted. This study was subsequently published in a Nashville

Tennessean article titled "Christians Can Believe in Bell Witch."[64] One of the reasons some Christians believe in witches is that they appear in the Bible, especially the Old Testament. The following is a partial list of biblical citations of witchcraft: I Chronicles 10:13, I Samuel 15:23, 28:15–19, II Chronicles 33:6, Leviticus 19:31, 20:6, 20:27, Revelation 18:23, 21:8, Galatians 5:19–21, Micah 5:10–12, Acts 19:17–20, 8:9-13, Isaiah 8:19–22, 19:1-4, 47:8–14, Deuteronomy 18:10–14.[65]

In 1961, R. A. Gray from Fayetteville, Tennessee, sent a letter to the *Nashville Banner* that explained why someone could believe in the Bible and the Bell Witch: "After reading The Bell Witch book we wonder what happened in Robertson County. Did such a thing ever happen before? We find in the Bible (which is THE best seller) that in chapter 28 of I Samuel that Saul went to the Witch of Endor to raise Samuel. So after reading the 'BW' and I Samuel, the whole thing becomes interesting."[66]

MY TEACHER SAID SO

Apologies to all social studies teachers, but history is one of the least favorite classes for many students. As a former history teacher, I draw this conclusion from personal experience. According to history teacher James W. Loewen, one reason for this attitude is that American history has been taught with "an embarrassing amalgam of bland optimism, blind patriotism, and misinformation pure and simple.[67] Disdain for the subject aside, research has shown that students have a propensity for believing, without question, what they are taught in school.

In a similar vein to our discussion of George Washington, Philip Deloria recently wrote about the misinformation in our Thanksgiving story.[68] Despite gross inaccuracies, the traditional story remains an important part of early education. As authority figures, teachers play a significant role in helping students develop their worldviews. What students are taught will likely stay with them for the rest of their lives; the viewpoints of their teachers will become an extension of their own beliefs. Therefore, what we are taught will become truth, whether it is or not.

PASCAL'S WAGER AND POST HOC, ERGO PROPTER HOC

Blaise Pascal's maintained that individuals wager whether there is a God. According to Pascal, logic and reason dictate that humans should always live their lives as if God exists. If they are wrong, there is no downside and Heaven awaits. But if they are wrong, and there is a God, Hell awaits. In simple terms, do not question if there is a God, live life as if there is a God.[69] Post hoc ergo propter hoc is Latin for "after this, therefore because of this." According to Michael Schermer, the human brain wants—and perhaps even needs—things to be neat, with no loose ends.[70] In a sense, the concept is an effect looking for a cause.[71]

If we modify Pascal's Wager to the "Bell Witch's Wager," both the wager and post hoc ergo propter hoc apply to the witch story. One of the foundational beliefs about the Bell Witch is that if you deny her existence, she will punish you. The punishment is demonstrative of post hoc, ergo propter hoc. In order to avoid the potential punishment of not believing in the Bell Witch, people are willing to accept that she not only exists but also exerts agency over their lives. Over one hundred years ago, George V. Triplett wrote an article for the *Louisville Courier-Journal* that supported this idea: "Any occurrence of an unusual nature, not assignable to a known cause afford . . . an opportunity to ascribe it to the agency of demons. In Tennessee, the recent history of the 'BW' seems to be a well-authenticated story of demonistic horrors."[72] Antithetical to the "Bell Witch's Wager, one the most popular examples of the Bell Witch denial concept is the "mirror story." Turn the lights off, light a candle, look in a mirror, and say some version of "I don't believe in the Bell Witch" three times. According to legend, the Bell Witch will appear and "get" you. To this day, some young people still do this stunt.[73]

The following is a true personal anecdote. In October 2019, the Robertson County Historical Society had its meeting in Adams on the grounds of the old Bell schoolhouse, not far from the Bell homeplace where the legend began. During my lecture, I denied any belief in the Bell Witch story and moved on to discuss the origins and circulation of the tale. My denial made some of the people in the audience visibly uneasy. During the next week, these things happened: my wife received over one hundred tick bites while working in the yard. The refrigerator quit working and had to be replaced. My daughter contracted a mild case of MRSA. Though my wife and I had tickets to see Old Crow Medicine Show at the Ryman Auditorium, we had to give our tickets away so we could take care of our grandson while our daughter recovered. Further, a storm blew a tree down blocking the road to our gravel bar on Red River, which meant I could not use the gravel bar to go kayaking. While I was cutting the tree to free the bar from the blockage, a log fell on my foot and broke two of my toes. A sensible person would argue that there are plenty of perfectly logical explanations for all these happenings. Tick bites occur when one does not use bug spray. Old refrigerators wear out over time and must be replaced. My daughter is a nurse, and on occasion encounters cases of MRSA while doing her job. Trees are regularly blown down in windstorms. Accidents happen and toes get broken. For many people, however, these things happened explicitly because I denied the Bell Witch. For them, these events were enacting a version of Pascal's Wager and post hoc, ergo propter hoc. Several believers asked me if I was now a believer too.

Two other superstitions pertaining to the Bell Witch deserve special attention. One such belief is that if you take a rock or other such trinkets out of the Bell Witch cave, she will punish you. Dr. Brandon Barker, assistant professor of Folklore and Ethnomusicology at Indiana University was raised in Middle Tennessee and grew up hearing Bell Witch stories. His mother knew the "rock" story and because of this tried to convince him not to come to Adams to do research on the Bell Witch. When he persisted, she told him to check his tires before he left Adams and to remove any rocks before he came home.[74]

The other notable superstition is that the Bell Witch does not like books being written or read about her. Books are said to have disappeared from libraries and people's homes. Most likely a result of this superstition, some library patrons burned books after reading them. One of many examples of this phenomena was featured in the *Paducah Sun* in 2004. The article reported that the Marshall Country library was going to "get tough" with patrons who did not return books. The books on the Bell Witch were the most frequently "lost."[75] These are just two of numerous similar articles that appeared in newspapers around the country.

PEOPLE ENJOY BEING SCARED

In a recent *Psychology Today* article, Dr. Christopher Dwyer lists five reasons that people like being scared:

1. The safety net: scared but safe.
2. The rush of adrenaline, endorphins and dopamine gives us a high.
3. Feeling good about facing our fears.

4. A shared experience/closeness to others.

5. Curiosity about the "dark side" and facing our fears.[76]

The Bell Witch story fosters all five of these criteria. According to the legend, the Spirit, as it was sometimes called, only killed one person, John Bell, and rarely hurt people outside the Bell family. We could be scared, but safe. There will be further discussion of these ideas when we explore Bell Witch movies.

CONFORMITY BIAS AND COMMUNAL NORMS

Conformity bias is fueled by the need of individuals to "conform with those around them, and when we are surrounded by peers who hold identical beliefs, the forces of conformity became extremely strong"[77]; or, to put it another way, "What you believe depends on who you know."[78] Yuval Harari uses this example to describe conformity bias. "Why do I believe . . . in a dollar bill? Because my neighbors believe in them."[79] The application of Harari's idea makes belief in the Bell Witch simple. People believe in the Bell Witch because their neighbors believe in the Bell Witch. The neighbors believe in the Bell witch because their own neighbors believe in the Bell Witch. In this way, the belief comes self-perpetuating and self-sustaining. Conformity bias helped various groups to develop communal norms at society's conception. These norms set the boundaries on individual actions and beliefs. Doing so made it easier for people to cooperate and build and maintain stable communities and, eventually, countries.

Belief in the Bell Witch became a communal norm in the settlement called Red River and later Adams, then in other areas of the United States as well. This point was supported by an unknown writer who sent this note to his local newspaper. In this section we talk about the Bell Witch as if she were a real person.[80] Please note the use of the word "we."

SUSPENSION OF DISBELIEF

Storytelling often requires the audience to suspend disbelief, whether they are reading a book, watching a movie or a play or listening to a storyteller live. We intrinsically know that popular superheroes and movie characters are not real. Even so, we enjoy consuming media and often identify with the characters as if they are real. Even people who do not necessarily believe in the Bell Witch can suspend their disbelief while watching a Bell Witch movie or live stage play, listening to a talented Bell Witch storyteller, or reading a compelling Bell Witch book. If only for a while, the Bell Witch is real, too.[81] Thus, the Bell Witch legend can be used as a paradigm to help us understand what and why people believe in things they cannot prove.

Throughout this chapter we have explored storytelling, especially about the Bell Witch. We have also considered what some people believe that they cannot prove to be true and why they believe such things, especially concerning the Bell Witch legend. It is time for us to examine the Bell Witch story itself.

.

two

THE LEGEND

Ode to Kate
By the dark of the night the goblin came,
And scratched upon the window pane,
With pointed nails right straight from hell,
She came to curse the name of Bell,
And tormented Old John right to his grave,
Before returning to her cave,
And from deep within this haunted den,
In seven years she came again,
And never would we be the same,
For something wicked this way came.

—DEWEY EDWARDS,
Something Wicked! The Bell Witch Phenomenon

PROLOGUE

In ancient Greek literature, a comedy had a happy ending even if some sad events occurred in the story. A tragedy had a sad ending even if happy scenes appeared in the story. The Bell Witch legend is a tragedy that includes some comedic events. The core of the saga begins with a scratch, a knock, and a whisper, and ends with a death.

There is not "a" Bell Witch legend: there are several versions with multiple variations. The three best-known renditions come from Tennessee, North Carolina, and Mississippi. Of the three, the version from Red River/Adams, Tennessee, is the best-known. (In 1850, Red River

Tennessee, was renamed Adams.) This iteration has produced dozens of books and essays, and hundreds of newspaper articles, plays, songs, and movies.[1] In this retelling of the story, I will focus on the Tennessee version, but include information about the North Carolina and Mississippi tales. I believe that the Bell Witch legend is one of the best-known pieces of folklore in American storytelling. Even so, I will write this summation as if it were true, as true as Homer's storytelling. As William Gay suggests in his Bell Witch article, "Here's what happened or maybe happened or is supposed to have happened."[2]

John Bell sold 360 acres of land in Edgecombe County, North Carolina, in October 1804. In late 1804 or early 1805, the Bell family moved to the Red River community close to present-day Adams, Tennessee. John Bell and his wife, Lucy Williams Bell, traveled with their six children, Jesse, John Jr., Drewry, Benjamin, Esther, and Zadoc. Elizabeth (Betsy), Richard Williams, and Joel Egbert were born after the relocation in Red River. They also brought enslaved people with them. The enslaved person who had the most encounters with the "spirit" was Dean.[3]

GENESIS

For over a decade, the Bell family had a good life in their new Tennessee home. They knew some of their neighbors from North Carolina and met families they had not known before. With the help of enslaved people, they cleared land and began farming. Three children were added to their flesh and blood line. And then life changed.

The first strange events began in 1817 and occurred outside the Bell house. This phenomenon transpired as John Bell was walking in a cornfield close to his home. He saw a dog unlike any he had ever seen before sitting in a cornrow looking at him. Because he did not recognize the animal, he raised his gun and shot at it. He felt sure that he had hit the creature. Even so, it ran off unharmed.

Not long afterward, Drewry also saw a strange-looking creature he had not seen before. It appeared to be a turkey, but larger than any turkey he had ever seen. He ran to the house and retrieved his gun. By the time he got back to the field, the extraordinary large fowl was flying away. In both cases, father and son assumed that because they were living in a new part of the world, it was logical that they would see animals that did not live in North Carolina.

And then Betsy saw the hanging girl. She made out a pretty young girl in a green dress swinging by her neck from a limb on an oak tree close to the house. She tried to communicate with the child but received no response. She went to the house to get family members to witness the sighting, but when they returned to the tree, the girl in the green dress was gone.

THE CURSED FAMILY

There was worse to come. Soon after the sightings, things began to happen in the Bell home. Family members began hearing strange sounds: soft whispering, slight knocking on doors and windows, choking and strangling, and gentle, rat-like scratching. They repeatedly searched for the source of the noises, especially when they grew louder and kept them awake at night. Even so, they could not discover the origin of the disturbances. Then things got worse. The rat's gnawing sounds started on their bed posts, which made it even harder to sleep. They heard wings flapping on the ceiling, chains being dragged across the floors, and loud, invisible dog fights inside the house. When family members finally fell sleep, their bed covers would be mysteriously pulled off each of them, especially Betsy.

Just when Bell family members thought things could not get worse, the physical abuse started. The "Spirit" as the malevolent entity came to be known was especially cruel to John Bell Sr. and Betsy. Joel and Richard Williams were tortured to a lesser degree. The Spirit was easier on John Jr. and showed affection and respect for Lucy. When it began verbally communicating with people, the Spirit said that Lucy was "the most perfect woman living."

The Spirit never gave a clear explanation for why she haunted the family, but it became clear that it hated John Bell and Betsy. The torture began in 1817 and continued until his death in 1820.

John Bell Sr.

As early as 1817, John Bell Sr. was abused both verbally and physically. The Spirit regularly called him "Old John Bell" and menaced him with profanity, curses, and threats. Soon after the haunting began, he started to have trouble speaking, eating, and swallowing. He said it felt like he had a stick of wood lodged between both cheeks in his mouth. This agony would plague him until his death. The Spirit often threatened John Bell Sr.; when asked why (after it began talking), the Spirit would answer, "Because he deserves killing." No further explanation was given.

Betsy Bell

Apart from her father, Betsy was subjected to the most torment. The Spirit would prick her with invisible pins and cause great pain. It would also slap Betsy until her face was red and drag her around the room by her hair. This abuse happened repeatedly. Combs would fly out of Betsy's hands and hair. The family was afraid that the Spirit would kill Betsy, and so sent her to friends' houses to spend the night. Many of these nights were spent at Theny Thorn's house. The haint would follow her to the Thorn household. Another trick it would play on Betsy was to untie her shoelaces and throw the shoes across the room. One night, Theny chided the entity for its actions. The Spirit responded with crude, loud laughter. An itinerate witch doctor gave Betsy a potion that would cure her from her affliction. Instead, Betsy vomited pins as the Spirit laughed.

Perhaps the cruelest thing the Spirit did to Betsy concerned her affection for Joshua Gardner. The Gardners were neighbors of the Bells, and Betsy and Joshua were sweethearts. When the Spirit found this out, it started chanting, "Please Betsy please, don't marry Joshua Gardner." This incantation went on for months and, out of fear, Betsy ended her relationship with Joshua. This encounter would become one of the best-known stories about the Bell Witch.

Joel and Richard Williams Bell

The haint did not pay much attention to Joel and Richard Williams, and only tormented them on occasion. It repeatedly pulled the covers off them, especially on cold nights and usually with a cackle. On one night, they were alone in their bedroom when the Spirit again pulled the covers off them. Joel lost his temper and spoke harshly to it. The Spirit spit on him, causing Richard Williams to utter angry words. Joel had to watch helplessly while the haint spanked his brother.

John Bell Jr.

John Jr. and the Spirit often had deep intellectual conversations. He often called the haint the "spirit of the Damned." Even so, the Spirit did not harm him. Instead, it would give him good advice, which he usually ignored. After a while, the Spirit would take a break from hurting the Bell family and would have conversations with them. On one occasion, John Jr. was discussing a trip by horseback he was going to take to North Carolina to settle some family business. The Spirit broke the conversation and told John Jr. that it would be a wasted trip as the matter had already been settled. She also advised him that a rich woman was on her way to Robertson County to visit friends. Because both were unmarried, they could meet and would make a good couple. He went anyway. The trip was wasted, and he might well have missed the love of his life. Maybe he should have listened.

Lucy Bell

When Lucy complained to the haint about its treatment of her family, it would reply that although it hurt her family it would never hurt her. When Lucy fell ill with pleurisy, an illness that made her bedridden and could have killed her, the Spirit talked to her in a soft, kind voice and brought her grapes even though they were out of season. It knew that Lucy loved to eat grapes. It would also drop grapes onto the bed when Lucy had company. The haint also knew that Lucy liked hazelnuts. It would drop nuts from the ceiling onto Lucy's bed. Lucy said that she could not eat the nuts because she could not crack them open. Immediately cracked nuts fell on the bed.

FRIENDS AND NEIGHBORS

John Bell would not allow his family members to talk to anyone outside the family about what was happening in their home. As the events increased in horror and pain, he finally realized that he needed to talk to someone. He chose to share information with his best friend and neighbor in the Red River community.

The Reverend James Johnston

That friend and neighbor was James Johnston. Bell confided in Johnston and invited him to spend the night at the Bell house to experience what the family had endured for what seemed like an eternity. Johnston arrived at the Bell home during the day and listened to the Bells recall the haunting. After it got dark, the candles in the room were doused by an unseen hand. A high-pitched scream filled the room, and Betsy received several hard slaps to her face. Reverend Johnston arose and, in a loud voice, said, "In the name of the Lord, what or who are you? What do you want and why are you here?" The questions went unanswered, and Betsy continued being slapped.

Johnston was shaken by the experience and implored John Bell Sr. to share the family's experiences with their neighbors and especially their church family. He believed that Satan or one of his demons from Hell was at work in the Bell home. After more hesitation, Bell and his family began to talk to people in the Red River community. As these conversations took place, a new name began to be used in the Red River community; then Robertson County; then the Tennessee and Kentucky counties surrounding Robertson County; then both states; then the United States; then the world. The phrase was "The Bell Witch."

LOCAL PEOPLE AND THE WITCH

Word spread rapidly in Red River and soon the Bell home was full of people on many nights as neighbors wanted to hear the Bell Witch talk. She was never visible but enjoyed having conversations. Some people reported their own experiences with the Bell Witch.

William Porter

Porter was a bachelor and spent several nights at the Bell home conversing with the Spirit. One night, the witch visited Porter at his home, climbed into his bed, and said, "Billy, I have come to sleep with you and to keep you warm." Porter told her that she "must behave yourself." Instead, she rolled herself up in all the covers leaving Porter to freeze. He grabbed up the covers and tried to throw her into the fireplace. Halfway across the room a horrible stench emerged from the covers. He dropped them and ran outside to breathe fresh air.

Frank Miles

In a similar experience, the haint visited Miles in his home and started snatching the blankets off him. He was a large, strong man weighting almost 250 pounds. He used all his strength to try to stay covered. The witch hit him several times.

John and Calvin Johnston

These young men were James Johnston's sons. They spent many nights conversing with the witch at the Bell house. One night, Calvin asked her if he could shake her hand. She refused at first, but then relented. Calvin reported that the hand was soft and feminine and had fingers. When John asked to shake her hand, she refused, saying that he was too clever and might try to catch her.

Drewry Bell and Bennett Porter

The witch repeatedly told local people about buried treasure in the area. She told Drewry and Bennett where they could uncover a large amount of money. The boys dug all day and found nothing. The witch and local citizens got a good laugh out of the boy's failed adventure. The witch pulled this trick on several other people in the area.

James Gunn

Gunn was the neighbor who had several conversations with the Bell Witch. She informed Gunn that she planned to torment "Old Jack" to his grave. When asked why, she would not give him a reason. But the poltergeist did share a piece of information that would change the course of the whole story. She identified herself as "Old Kate Batts' witch." From then on, the witch was often called "Kate."

Kate Batts

Mary Catherine "Kate Batts" and her husband, Frederick, were neighbors of the Bells. Kate was well-known in Red River as an "eccentric" character. When she met someone, she would ask them if she could borrow a pin. According to local superstitions, if a person loaned a pin to someone, it gave the receiver a measure of control over the lender. This trait and others irritated many local people including the Bells. Even so, Kate's relationship with John Bell, Sr. was more severe. Although Kate had a husband, she was the leader of the family. She took Bell to court charging that he had cheated her family on the sale of an enslaved person. Her behavior led many local people to believe that she was the witch or was in control of the witch.

RELIGION

The Bell Witch liked to discuss and sometimes argue about religion with visitors at the Bell house. One of her favorite things to do was ask to her audience to recite quotes from the Bible. After each quote, she would identify the chapter and verse. She was never wrong. After Revered Johnston's first visit to the Bell home, Kate started calling him "Old Sugarmouth" and would repeat last Sunday's sermon for the audience. In an added attempt to irritate "Old Sugarmouth," she would start speaking in his voice. One of her best-known stunts was to recite the sermon that Reverend James Gunn gave at the local Methodist Church and then recite the sermon Pastor Suggs Fort gave at the local Baptist Church. Both sermons were given at the same time at churches thirteen miles apart.

FOUR SPIRITS

To make life even harder, four of the witch's spirit friends arrived at the Bell farm. Each entity had its own personality and physical features. Each had a feminine voice, but with different tones. Blackdog, the leader of the group, had a harsh voice. Mathematics and Cypocryphy had softer voices, and Jerusalem had a child's voice. The five of them used foul language and spent extensive periods quarreling with each other. Sometimes they were in Red River and other times they were gone. Even so, the Bell family lived in fear that they would return.

DEAN

The Bell Witch had a particular dislike of Black people. She tormented and beat them almost daily and did not want the enslaved people who worked outside to come into the house. An enslaved person named Dean had several conflicts with Kate and survived them all. He often had conflicts with the haint in the form of a large black dog, which sometimes had one head or two heads or was headless. He also claimed that she once turned him into a mule. He was attacked so many times that his wife made him a "witch ball" to protect him, and he always carried an ax with him.

Dean had a favorite witch story that he liked to recount. One day, after his work was finished, he and his dog Caesar were going to visit his wife, who was enslaved on a neighboring farm. He felt safe because Kate was busy with visitors in the Bell house. He was hoping to find a possum he could take back home with him. Caesar treed a possum and Dean put it on the ground and pulled its tail through a split stick. Dean heard a noise and turned around to see a giant rabbit. The rabbit freed the possum and told Dean he would teach him to never put another possum's tail in a split stick. Then the rabbit hit Dean on the head with a large stick. He did not wake up until the morning. When telling the story, Dean would show the listeners his head scar and declare that he would never again put a possum's tail in a split stick.

VISITORS

If there was anyone the Bell Witch disliked more than the enslaved, it was outsiders coming to Red River. It was as if they were invading her domain.

The Shakers

The Shakers were a sect of Christianity known for its ecstatic worship ceremonies that included frenzied noises and whirling. The Shakers were also known for being industrious and inventing better versions of existing items. There was a Shaker community in Kentucky not far from Red River. Although Shakers were known to be good, industrious people, Kate did not like them. On occasion, a group of Shaker traders would arrive at the Bell home, where they were treated with hospitality. Kate decided to put an end to their visits to Red River. Dean and his brother Harry had three dogs, Caesar, Tiger, and Bulger. She sicced the dogs on the Shakers. They never returned.

Dr. Mize

Mize was a noted wizard or conjurer in Franklin, Kentucky, not far from the Bell farm. He claimed to be able to drive unwanted spirits from a home. Drewery Bell and James Johnston went to Franklin to convince him to come to Red River and force the Bell Witch to quit tormenting the Bell family. He came with great confidence that he could control the witch. She cursed and mocked him and laughed at his failed efforts to remove her from the house. The next morning, he left saying that she knew more about witchcraft than he did.

Mr. Williams

Williams claimed to be a trained detective and had traveled a great distance to investigate the alleged haunting of the Bell home. He did not believe in supernatural events and bragged that he could uncover the hoax. He spent several uneventful days in the Bell home. Then one night while Williams was in bed, the Spirit beat and cursed at him, demeaning his supposed skills. He left the next morning without eating breakfast.

General Andrew Jackson

Jackson was the most famous of all the people who came to the Bell farm to investigate the events occurring there. John Bell Jr. had fought with Jackson at the Battle of New Orleans during the War of 1812. Jackson remembered this, and when he heard about the supernatural events happening in Red River, he decided to go investigate. He lived at the Hermitage close to Nashville and about thirty-five miles from Red River. It took him and his party a couple of days to get to the Bell house.

But it was hard to get there. When Jackson's party got to the boundary of the Bell's property, the wheels on the carriages would not turn. The horses and mules pulled as hard as they could, but the carriages would not move. After a while, Kate's voice said, "Alright General, the wagons can move on." That night, Kate drank, sang, cursed, destroyed items in the house, and pulled the covers off anyone who tried to go to sleep. Early the next morning as Jackson and his party were leaving the Bell farm, the general said, "I would rather fight the British ten times over than to ever face the Bell Witch again."

WHO ARE YOU, AND WHY ARE YOU HERE?

After the Bell Witch began conversing with people, she was repeatedly asked these two questions. From 1817 until 1820, Kate gave several different answers. Some were:

- "I am a spirit; I was once very happy but I have been disturbed."
- "I was the spirit of an Indian who had once lived in the area."
- "I am the spirit of an immigrant who buried treasure under a large rock on the banks of the river and I want Elizabeth Bell to have it."
- "I am the spirit of a person who was buried in the woods nearby and the grave was disturbed, my bones disinterred and scattered, and one of my teeth was lost under the house. I am looking for the tooth."
- "I am a spirit from everywhere, Heaven, Hell, the earth, the air, the houses, any place at any time. I was created millions of years ago."

Although Kate offered several versions that she was haunting the Bell house, there was one explanation she repeatedly gave: "I have come to kill John Bell." And she did.

LAMENTATIONS

John Bell suffered from Kate's cruelty for almost four years without knowing why the witch tortured him physically, emotionally, and psychologically. Sometimes the abuse was constant, followed by periods of rest and quiet. By December 1820, Bell was so sick that he could not eat or get out of bed. He died of poisoning on December 20, 1820. As he was dying, Kate cackled, "I have got him this time; he will never get up from the bed this time." At John Bell's funeral, the Bell Witch could be heard singing bawdy drinking songs. She repeatedly said, "Roll me out some brandy, oh roll, roll, roll, roll. Roll me out some brandy, oh roll me out some more."

EXODUS

In the years after John Bell's death, several family members left Robert-son County. It was a common pattern during the era for people to leave what had been home to start over in other areas. This was especially true for migrants headed to Native American territory that was being opened to white settlers. Joshua Gardner and other Robertson County residents migrated to west Tennessee, which had recently been opened to settle-ment. In the Bell family, new land in Mississippi was the chosen state for Lucy, Betsy, and Esther. Zadoc Bell ended up in Alabama. The migration pattern for the Bells and Gardners was similar for other families in Rob-ertson and surrounding counties.

SO, IS THE STORY TRUE?

People have been arguing and debating this question since John Bell was alive. Writer William Gay sums up the possible answers to this question as follows: Everyone who went looking for a solution found one, so there are ultimately more answers than questions and more culprits than victims.

1. It was a hoax perpetrated by Betsy Bell for reasons unknown, possibly a prank. She acquired the art of ventriloquism and put it to use.
2. It was a hoax perpetrated by one Richard Powell, who wanted to get rid of Joshua Gardner and John Bell and marry into the well-to-do Bell family.
3. It's true as told, and in the world as we know it there is no explanation.
4. Something happened, a poltergeist perhaps, but it's been grossly distorted by time and retelling.
5. It was black magic. Kate Batts *was* a witch, and this was her revenge on John Bell.
6. The Bell farm is located on an ancient source of power, sacred to the Indians and whatever race came before them. Spirits have always been there, and they sometimes draw on energy wherever they can find it. According to theories about poltergeists, an unhappy household filled with adolescents would provide an almost inexhaustible supply of energy. (It

might be worth pointing out that the spirit's powers waned
as Betsy passed from adolescence to womanhood.)[4]

Maybe one or none of Gay's suggestions is true. A perusal of Bell Witch
websites and podcasts produces numerous theories. Even so, one thing
is true: the people who left Robertson and surrounding counties to live
in other parts of the country took their versions of the story with them.
Those who decided to stay in the area had their versions as well. In each
case, people told the Bell Witch story.

Moving on from the legend itself, we cannot grasp the development
and growth of the Bell Witch story without understanding the religious,
social, and cultural environment in Robertson and surrounding counties
in the early 1800s. The story developed in the period between the Second Great Awakening and the Spiritualism Movement. The Second Great
Awakening was a Protestant religious revival that had some of its strongest
influence in the frontier regions of Kentucky and Tennessee from the late
1790s until the 1820s. The movement spread in part through revivals and
emotional preaching. The religious gatherings took the form of camp
meetings, often with hundreds of people attending and lasting for days.[5]
Two of the largest revivals took place at the Red River Meeting House in
Logan County, Kentucky, and Cane Ridge, Kentucky. The Cane Ridge
revival took place in August 1801 and attracted twenty thousand people.[6]

These religious revival meetings, in conjunction with circuit-riding
preachers, caused Protestant church memberships to rise quickly. Many
worshippers came to religion for the first time and were baptized. Even so,
some people were worried about what they witnessed at the revivals and
church meetings. In the throes of religious fervor, worshippers exhibited
aberrant behavior. Participants went into trances, had the "jerks," laughed
uncontrollably, spoke in tongues, barked like dogs, and other behaviors
that were unusual by previous religious norms.[7] Historian Herman A.
Norton called this behavior "acrobatic Christianity."[8]

Some observers of these behaviors saw them as proof of the presence
of the Holy Spirit at the meetings, while other witnesses interpreted the
events as evidence that Satan was at work. In his book on the Cane Ridge
revival, historian Paul Conkin quotes an observer at the revival: "The most
exorcised were literally possessed by evil spirits, and that the so-called
revival, among those who had departed from scriptural worship by the introduction of human-created hymns, was a work of Satan."[9] Another viewer

declared, "We can assume that Satan, or the Devil, held a very prominent place in the popular understanding of what happened at Cane Ridge.[10]

In his autobiography, Methodist minister Peter Cartwright recorded that the revivals in Cane Ridge were "Satan's work versus God's work." He reported that some people were "mortified by the 'jerks' and that two brothers threatened to horsewhip him for giving their sister 'the jerks.'"[11] The jerks occurred when a person overwhelmed by emotion fell to the floor and spasmed uncontrollably. A contemporary Baptist preacher, Elder Reuben Ross, described what was called the falling exercise, the jerks, the dancing exercise, the barking exercise, the laughing exercise, and the singing exercise. He quoted another Baptist leader, Elder Hoge, who, while watching a revival, said, "We can do nothing. If it be of Satan, it will soon come to an end; but if it be of God, our efforts and fears are in vain."[12] Ross also wrote about hearing stories in his childhood from his grandmother and other adults pertaining to witches and other supernatural entities. He reported that many of the storytellers "were very superstitious and could tell marvelous tales of witches, ghosts, and apparitions, to which as a boy, I listened with great interest." He heard stories about witches who tormented local citizens and who could take the shape of animals.[13]

The early 1800s in frontier Kentucky and Tennessee was a time of surging religious beliefs among many citizens. It was also an era when many people also believed in witches, ghosts, and other supernatural events. Thus, many local inhabitants who heard of the strange events happening at the Bell house believed that supernatural events were in fact occurring. Therefore, it is reasonable to conclude that as religion evolved on the frontier, these beliefs and traditions directly contributed to the genesis of the Bell Witch story.

The concurrent belief in both Christianity and the Bell Witch is still prevalent in the town of Adams and Robertson County. Further research would undoubtedly reveal a symbiotic relationship between Christianity and the supernatural in other regions as well. On Halloween Day, 2006, the *Nashville Tennessean* published an article concerning Adams, entitled, "Christians Can Believe in Bell Witch, Town Says." The article quoted a local preacher saying, "As a Christian, we recognize angels as being messengers of God and demons being messengers from dark sources, from Satan, the devil." A prominent Robertson County citizen supplied this quote: "Certainly the Old Testament is full of encounters with spirits and oracles. And then, of course, the New Testament clearly has the discouragement of becoming involved with witchcraft and the occult." A prominent Adams resident added, "If you believe in the Bible, there are spirits walking around. The dead got up and walked. Some folks come back and forth. If you read that, it's not a stretch, Christians can believe in this and not be far off from what the Bible teaches." According to a Baptist-affiliated Baylor University poll, people in the South are more likely to believe in haunted houses than residents in the rest of the country.[14]

In the early 1800s, religious faith and belief in the supernatural could clearly coexist in the minds of local citizens. Current religious ethos demonstrates that this "coexistence" has survived and thrives to present day, which helps us understand how the Bell Witch story endured and grew over the two hundred years since its beginning. To better understand the story's endurance, it is equally important to recognize that the early 1800s was a time of both fear and hope, depending on how each individual interpreted the events of the era. At many points in history, this epoch included, people have either feared or welcomed the "apocalypse" or end of the world. Some people viewed the apocalypse as a time when knowledge would be revealed; others believed it foreshadowed the physical return of Jesus on earth, as prophesied in the Bible. Still others took a darker view, believing that the event would be cataclysmic and would bring about earth's complete destruction.[15]

Several events converged in the early 1800s that contributed to apocalyptic views. One such event was what became known as the "Great Comet of 1811."[16] In Leo Tolstoy's classic novel *War and Peace*, one of the characters describes the comet as a warning of "all kinds of woes and the end of the world."[17] The following year, a series of massive earthquakes, which became known as the New Madrid earthquakes, hit along the Mississippi River on the western borders of Tennessee and Kentucky. The effects were felt throughout the mid-South, including, of course, Robertson County. Many inhabitants interpreted the event as a sign from God that they needed to repent their sinful ways and that the end times were near. Many churches reported a surge in membership, at least until the crisis abated.[18]

One religious leader used this poem to warn people to repent:

> The prophets did foretell of old,
> That great events are coming;
> The lord Almighty's bringing on
> The days of tribulation

Prepare, before it is too late,
To meet the Lord from heaven;
King Jesus stands with open arms,
To save your souls from ruin.[19]

Add to these events a long-standing memory of conflict with Native Americans and the War of 1812, and it becomes easy to understand the pervasive uncertainty and anxiety that contributed to religious revival on the frontier.

People living in the region that produced the Bell Witch story shared these concerns with other Americans. Methodist preacher and circuit rider Peter Cartwright called Logan County, Kentucky, "Rogues' Harbor" and contended that the country was full of "murderers, horse thieves, highway robbers, and counterfeiters."[20] Logan County was on the Tennessee border, a few miles from the Red River settlement. He also wrote that "the earthquakes struck terror to thousands of people and under the mighty panic hundreds and thousands crowded to and joined the different churches."[21] Reuben Ross, a Baptist minister who preached in the same general area as Cartwright, called the new converts to religion "earthquake Christians."[22] He also told the story of "Old Brother" Valentine Cook who, when the first earthquake hit, jumped out of bed and ran down the street shouting, "My Lord is coming! My Lord is coming!" He also recorded that in 1811–1812, the combination of "Indians, war, comets and earthquakes . . . were beginning to cast their shadows before and to fill the public mind with forebodings of trouble."[23]

Evolving religious practice, unusual cosmic and geological events, and the influence of itinerant preachers on the frontier all contribute to our understanding of the environment that fostered the Bell Witch lore. Historian Jason Bivins wrote, "Impulses to identify and purge witches peak during periods of anxiety, unrest and demographic change."[24] This perfectly describes the frontier region of Tennessee and Kentucky in the first two decades of the 1800s. A better understanding of the story's origins now allows us to turn our attention to exactly how the story endured and spread.

three

ORAL TRANSMISSION

Language is very powerful. Language
does not just describe reality.
Language creates the reality it describes.

—DESMOND TUTU,
Good Reads

Sing in me, muse, and through me
tell the story . . .

—HOMER,
The Odyssey

Never let the truth get in the way of a good story.

—ATTRIBUTED TO MARK TWAIN

Homo sapiens can speak about things that
don't really exist, and believe six impossible
things before breakfast.

—HARARI,
Sapiens

The Bell Witch will survive as long as storytelling exists.

—*LOUISVILLE COURIER-JOURNAL,*
October 6, 1973

> After nourishment, shelter, and companionship,
> stories are the thing we need the most in the world.
>
> —PHILLIP PULLMAN,
> *Daemon Voices*

> Language creates reality.
>
> —MICHEL FOUCAULT

This chapter is a continuation of the discussion in Chapter 1 on storytelling with a focus on the Bell Witch legend. I do not remember a time before I knew the Bell Witch story. Storytelling was a major part of entertainment when I was a child and then an adult. One of my uncles would say, "Boy, remember, do not let the truth get in the way of a good story." The importance was the story, not the truth. One of my great uncle's favorite sayings was, "Boy, there ain't nothin' better'n a good story cep'n a mother's love and Tennessee whiskey."

Both of my relatives were following a pattern set thirty-thousand years ago when humans learned to speak. As mentioned earlier in this narrative, possibly humans learned to speak so they could tell stories.[1] Maybe humans have a compulsion to tell stories. Highly successful novelist Richard Russo wrote, "We tell stories because we must."[2] The same is true for the receiver of the story. We must hear stories. I would rather someone tell me a good story than buy me a good meal. I can buy a good meal, but it takes another person to tell me a good story that I do not know. Of course, both at the same time would be best.

Stories help sapiens understand the relationship between the past, present, and the future. In his novel on the Vietnam War, novelist Tim O'Brien wrote that "Stories are for joining the past to the future."[3] At the same time, stories can anchor people in a time and place and open a portal to another world. In short, stories do more than entertain us and offer a way to pass time. They teach us.

Before we turn our attention to the oral transmission of the Bell Witch, we need to understand why some stories are more compelling than others. This will help us grasp how the Bell Witch legend became one of the most remembered stories in American and maybe even world folklore.

In a 1957 article on folk ballads, Tristram Coffin opined that to be successful and remembered a folk ballad needed to meet four markers: action, character, setting, and theme.[4] The same is true for many stories. The Bell Witch hits all four markers. For action, the story has a haunting and a murder. The legend has several interesting characters including a witch. The setting is a frontier settlement far away from the comforts of urban life. Later in the story a cave will become important as a supernatural site. One of the many themes of the legend is that if you deny that the witch is real, she will "get you."

Another important goal a story must achieve is to arouse some of the listener's core emotions—happiness, sadness, fear, disgust, anger, and excitement or surprise, the emotions most humans share and that spark human responses to life experiences.[5] Some of these core emotions are what the listeners want to feel when they hear a story and what the storyteller wants them to feel. Now that we have reviewed storytelling in general, let us turn out attention to how oral transmission worked to spread the Bell Witch legend.

PATTERNS

The Bell Witch story fit perfectly into a major pattern of folktales. B. A. Botkin wrote that, "Tales of ghosts, witches, and the devil make up a large class of folktales based on superstitions, in which the story has often outlived the practice or belief."[6] A good example of Botkin's point is the similarities between the Tennessee Bell Witch story and the North Carolina Old Nance haunting, the Beaver story. Recall the Bell haunting from the previous chapter and compare it to the experiences of the Beaver family. According to the story, the following were true:

- Nobody saw Old Nance but could hear her.
- In the beginning of the haunting, she appeared on occasion and then almost every day.
- She pulled the covers off family members in the middle of the night.
- She ridiculed preachers who visited the Beaver home to investigate the haunting.
- She called some of the male visitors "Old Sugarmouth."
- She liked Sairy Beaver and brought her out of season fruit and berries when she was sick.

43

- She would visit churches to argue religion.
- She hated the father of the Beaver family, called him "Old Leatherhead," and declared that she would kill him.
- She had a screeching laughter and claimed she was upset because someone had dug up her bones.[7]

The depiction of the Beaver poltergeist is almost identical to the Bell Witch. This leaves us with a conundrum. Which story came first? The Bell Witch haunting story was 1817–1820, and the Miles book was published in 1905 with no dates for the Beaver visitation. Thus, who borrowed from whom? Did the Bell family bring the story with them from North Carolina, or did Miles borrow from the Bell Witch story, as published in M. V. Ingram's 1894 book? Or did both borrow from a pattern of haunting stories prevalent in various places around the world?

Another pattern that the Bell Witch legend blended into was the "mirror story." In a sentence: go into a dark room, light a candle, look into a mirror, and chant a short phrase designed to get a supernatural entity to appear in the mirror.[8] Probably the best-known of the mirror stories is "Bloody Mary." As is the case with the Bell Witch, popular culture includes numerous films, plays, television programs, and books about this folklore. A brief perusal of Wikipedia will provide the reader with an abundant amount of information on this subject.[9]

There are two version of the Bell Witch incantation. One is to stand in front of a mirror in a dark room with a candle burning and say three times, "I hate the Bell Witch." In the other rendition, the person says, "I don't believe in the Bell Witch." In either case, the witch will appear in the mirror. I was born and live in Robertson County and can attest to the fact that this act still occurs in the county, especially with middle and high school students.

There has been a more recent addition to the mirror stories. In October 2021, I was the guest storyteller at Historic Rugby's "Ghostly Gathering" during Halloween. Rugby is a picturesque British village in rural East Tennessee. I was speaking about the Bell Witch legend and asked the audience if anyone had ever heard of the mirror story. Quickly, a young man about ten years old shot his hand into the air. I asked him how he knew the story. He hollered out with one word: "Candyman!" There have been two versions of the film, one in 1992 and the other in 2019. The second film grossed $77 million worldwide.[10]

In both examples, patterns in the mirror story serve as a source for oral transmission of the Bell Witch legend. Each generation in Western North Carolina passed down the "Old Nance" story to the next generation. Generations in Tennessee and other states did the same for the Bell Witch folklore. The mirror stories followed the same template.[11] This pattern of generational oral transmission of the Bell Witch story continued even when people left Western North Carolina and Red River, Tennessee. This concept will be the core of the next part of this chapter.

PEOPLE TOOK THE STORY WITH THEM

After the death of John Bell in 1820, several Bell family members and neighbors left Red River, Tennessee. Zadoc Bell became a lawyer and moved to Montgomery, Alabama. Several Robertson County, Tennessee, families migrated to Panola and Yalobusha counties in Mississippi. They included Elizabeth (Betsy) Bell Powell and family, Esther Bell Porter and family, and the family of Martha Lee Gunn. Joshua Gardner, whom the Bell Witch would not allow to marry Betsy Bell, moved to Weakley County in West Tennessee along with other people from Red River.

Wherever people from Red River went, many of them carried the Bell Witch story with them. As discussed earlier, in an era before modern technology, people talked to each other and told their stories to educate and entertain. Vanderbilt professor Donald Davidson captured this concept in a 1928 article. Responding to a famous Will Rogers quote, he wrote: "All I know is that what I read in the papers has obscured and dwarfed valuable faculties that the illiterate cherish—faculties that belong as definitely to the field of culture as philosophy, art and literature. Singing, dancing, and telling of tales once was common, in the sense that they belonged to and were practiced by all the people."[12] In part, Davidson was supporting the importance of oral transmission.

Davidson also praised Arthur Palmer Hudson's role in spreading the Mississippi Bell Witch stories in his book *Specimens of Mississippi Folk-Lore*.[13] It is logical that as the Bells and other people from Robertson County moved to the same two counties in Mississippi, they brought the Bell Witch stories with them. It is also reasonable that local storytellers in Yalobusha and Panola counties would develop their versions of entertaining Bell Witch stories and set the stories in their own counties.

As Davidson praised Hudson's work, he could not resist the temptation to remind him of the true geographic origin of the Bell Witch legend. He ended his article on this note, "On only one point can I pick Professor Hudson up. The Bell Witch story, which he finds floating around in Mississippi, I must claim for Robertson County, Tennessee; if he will visit Springfield or Cedar Hill, he can dig up more material about the Bell Witch and her native haunts than he will know what to do with."[14] Six years later, Hudson, in conjunction with Pete Kyle McCarter, published a well-received article on the Bell Witch folk legend in both states. In their conclusion, they wrote:

> There is little doubt that some Mississippi communicants of the legend knew of Ingram's book in a vague and general way . . . The Bell family concerned lived in Mississippi; its descendants still live in the state.
>
> The independent development of the main outlines of the legend in Mississippi is along the lines of oral tradition. The variations, though suggested, perhaps, in some particulars, by the Tennessee version, take place in a direction not to be accounted for by the main outlines or the chief intention of the Tennessee story.[15]

Their conclusion is logical and supports the importance of orally transmitting the Bell Witch folk legend.

Two thoughts before we turn out attention from Mississippi to North Carolina. One, not long ago I had a conversation about the Bell Witch legend with a woman from Mississippi. She concluded the talk with these words: "Rick, the Bell Witch belongs to Mississippi!" Second, Betsy Bell's grave is in a cemetery close to Water Valley, Mississippi. Her grave marker includes these words:

ELIZABETH POWELL

BORN

IN ROBERTSON COUNTY, TENN

JAN 1806

DIED IN YALOBUSHA CO., MISS

JULY 11, 1888

A LOVED ONE HAVE GONE FROM CIRCLE

WE SHALL MEET HER NO MORE SHE

HAS GONE TO HER HOME IN HEAVEN

AND ALL HER AFFLICTIONS ARE OVER[16]

I wonder what her afflictions were.

Earlier in this chapter, we reviewed the North Carolina "Beaver Family" haunting and its commonalities with the Bell Witch. Over the last few decades, a new genre of Bell Witch stories has developed out of North Carolina that has little to do with the oral transmission of the story.[17]

EARLY BELL WITCH BOOKS
AND ORAL TRANSMISSION

M. V. Ingram's book, *An Authenticated History of the Bell Witch*, is the foundational source for the legend. In the preface of the narrative, he explains, "It might be a strange story, nevertheless, it is authentic" and was transmitted by the present generation of the surrounding country through family reminiscences of the most eventful and exciting period of the century, which set hundreds of people to investigating.[18] At the end of the book, he included sixty-nine pages of oral recollections and testimonials from people who had heard the stories from credible sources.[19] Ingram included Richard Williams Bell's manuscript "Our Family Trouble" in his book as a way to convince readers that the story was true. He was a descendant of John Bell.[20] Harriet Parks Miller published *The Bell Witch of Middle Tennessee* in 1930. Miller was a native of the area that produced the Bell Witch folklore, and as the quote at the beginning of this chapter suggests, she heard about the story from "reliable people."[21]

Charles Bailey Bell put "A Descendant" on the cover of his book *The Bell Witch of Tennessee*." He also claimed that "wherever he has been from California to the East coast, down in Mexico, in the South or North, he has been asked if he was one of the "Bell Witch" family.[22] His statement supports that the Bell Witch folklore had transcended Tennessee. Charles Bailey Bell also wrote that, "The author shall relate in this book what was handed down to him by his father, Dr. J.T. Bell, he having the recollections of his father, John Bell, Jr.,"[23] which would make him John Bell's great grandson. It is clear that oral transmission of the stories from generation to generation helped make the Bell Witch legend one of the best-known in the supernatural genre.

About the same time as the Miller and Charles Bailey Bell books were published, the Nashville Tennessean published an article about a ninety-five-year-old woman who remembered hearing Bell Witch stories when she was young. She was born in 1842, and heard the stories from people who remembered the haunting. After she married, she lived in a farmhouse within "a stone's throw from the old Bell house" and said that she never believed the stories. W. B. Williams, who wrote the article, declared, "It is clear from my research that many of the neighbors didn't believe in the 'Bell Witch' during the time of the legend. Today, there are those in the Adams community that do not believe the story as told by M. V. Ingram in 1894, but the legend still causes the hair to go up on the necks of many other people in Adams who believe the story is true."[24]

ENSLAVED NARRATIVES

The Bells and other white families were not the only people who used oral transmission to keep the Bell Witch folklore alive. Black families did as well. In the decades before the Civil War, the Wessyngton Plantation owned by George Washington was one of the largest plantations in Tennessee. Over two hundred enslaved people worked on the plantation in Robertson County not far from where the Bell Witch folklore originated. John F. Baker Jr., a descendant of enslaved ancestors at Wessyngton, wrote a history of the plantation on which the people were bound in involuntary servitude. He suggested that Black and White people both heard about the Bell Witch stories from the nearby Bell property. He added that stories about Dean, an enslaved man on the Bell farm, and the Bell Witch were prominent stories among the Wessyngton enslaved.[25]

Enslaved narratives about encounters with the Bell Witch were recorded in early books. Chapter 10 of Ingram's book is titled "Negro Stories." Richard Williams Bell included a chapter called "The Witch and the Negroes." Miller wrote about stories of enslaved people. Charles Baily Bell's book contained a chapter called "Recollections Given by Some of the Slaves."[26] Some of the most repeated stories concern an enslaved man named Dean. The witch repeatedly tortured him. Two of the most oft-repeated stories were the witch turning Dean into a mule and the time she "bursied" him in the head. The fact that some of the stories originating from the enslaved were among the most told accounts—and that they were told by Black people at Wessyngton—indicates that the oral tradition of passing Bell Witch stories transcended race and social position.

ACADEMIA

The 1970s were a period of renewed academic interest in folklore and the Bell Witch legend. Western Kentucky University launched a new MA program in folk studies in 1970.[27] Several of the students became interested in the Bell Witch folklore and wrote papers on the subject. Although the Bell Witch was a favorite topic of several students, I will focus on one as an example of the research students conducted, though all of these studies are housed in the university's Folklife Archives in the Special Collections Library.

Joseph Petrocelli, a student in one of the folk studies classes, was from Woodlynne, New Jersey, and chose to research the Bell Witch folklore. He came to Adams, which was about fifty miles from the university in Bowling Green and interviewed several local people about the subject. Most of his interviewees were from the area and relayed to him stories that they had been told. The following are just a few of the Bell Witch stories that he heard that originated two hundred years ago:

- The witch tormented Betsy Bell.
- She would make knocking sounds at night.
- It could take the shape of animals.
- She would cause a scene at local churches.
- John Bell shot at a strange animal and missed.
- It would jerk the covers off Bell family members in the middle of the night.
- Her grave was disturbed.
- It killed John Bell.
- Andrew Jackson came to Adams and met the witch.[28]

About the same time, students from Indiana University also became interested in the Bell Witch folklore. In 1972, they interviewed several local people about the legend. Some people spoke about Bell Witch events in modern times—especially stories concerning the Bell Witch cave. Other interviewees told stories they had heard from parents, grandparents, and great-grandparents. These stories were very similar to those reported by students from Western Kentucky University in 1970. Some of the related stories were:

- The witch pulled covers off people.
- She hated John Bell.
- She loved his wife.
- Weird noises at night

- Kate Batts was the witch.
- Preachers came to the Bell home to investigate the poltergeist.
- The Jackson story
- She visited churches.
- Besty Bell did not marry Joshua Gardner.[29]

Ralph Winters, a local historian and one of the people interviewed, reported that he had been told that Charles Bailey Bell was "needing money"
when he wrote his Bell Witch book.[30]

We have reviewed university academics who came to Adams in the
1970s to investigate the Bell Witch folklore. During this period, some
students at Tennessee universities brought their legends with them when
they entered the college. My wife went to Middle Tennessee State University in the 1970s. The school is seventy miles from Adams. When some
students found out that she was from Robertson County, they told her the
Bell Witch of MTSU stories. She was warned not to write a paper about
the Bell Witch. According to one of the tales, a girl wrote a paper about
the Bell Witch. A few days later, she hanged herself in her dorm room.
This is just one of several cautionary tales about the witch that she heard
at MTSU.

The Bell Witch stories were prominent on campus as late as 2017, and
maybe still are. A 2017 article appeared in an MTSU publication entitled
"Legends in Lyon: The Bell Witch Incident at MTSU." According to the
story, an MTSU student conducted a family history project for her class in
1968 and discovered she was a descendant of the Bell family. The story of
what happened to her has many variations, all of which end with the her
killing herself or being killed by the Bell Witch. The 2017 story is similar
to the one my wife heard on campus forty years ago.[31]

Academics and college students are not the only people keeping the
Bell Witch story alive, so are the people in Adams and elsewhere. On a
March day in 2022, I spend the day in Moss's Restaurant asking people
about their memories of the Bell Witch. The restaurant is in the old Bell
school building which also houses the Adams Museum and Archives. The
museum contains several Bell Witch lore items and regularly receives visitors inquiring about the poltergeist. Timothy Henson, a local historian
and author of a Bell Witch book, is the caretaker of the museum and is
usually there to answer their questions. I also visited him at the museum
and talked with visitors.

I am not going to mention anyone by name but will report that many people still believe that Old Kate does not like people talking about her. When I asked, "How and when did you learn about the Bell Witch?" I often got similar answers. The most common was that someone of an earlier generation told them. This was true when I talked not only to local people but also with visitors from Samford, North Carolina, Oxford, Mississippi, and Western Kentucky. When I asked: "How long have you known this folklore?" Often the answer was simple, "I don't remember not knowing the Bell Witch story."

I did hear two stories that fit the pattern from early Bell Witch lore. One woman from Robertson County told the story of her grandfather taking tobacco to market on a wagon pulled by mules. All at once, the mules stopped and refused to move forward. Next, the reins fell off the mules. The grandfather yelled, "Witch, leave my mules alone!" And she did.

Another local woman told a similar story. Her grandfather was walking one day when he noticed that he was being followed by a panther. He knew that the haint was known for her ability to take the shape of an animal. He hollered, "Damn it, Kate, I ain't bother you, so leave me alone." She did. Both stories are similar to the Andrew Jackson and other stories from almost two hundred years ago.

A story does not have to be true to be good. It needs to be well-told. It also helps if it connects to stories and beliefs that the listener already possesses. The Bell Witch saga meets both criteria, which contributes to why the stories have been told for over two hundred years and will continue to be heard. But we must also remember that the story was not only heard, but also read. This issue will be the topic of the next chapter.

four

SURVIVAL AND GROWTH,
1820–1894

The strange story of the Bell Witch of Robertson
County which has been floating around in an
indefinite shape for three quarters of a century has at
last been written out and publish in book form.

—REVIEW OF INGRAM'S *Authenticated History*,
Nashville Tennessee Banner, June 9, 1894

The writer is aware that the enlightened age of the
Twentieth century forbids belief in witches. In defense
of what will be said in the following pages, I will say
that my data has been secured from reliable people,
some of whom visited the Bell home, and went
away mystified as to what they saw and heard, and
in consequence thereof they found it impossible to
dismiss the whole thing as a delusion or hallucination.

—HARRIET PARKS MILLER,
The Bell Witch of Middle Tennessee

There are very few people in Middle Tennessee
who don't know about the Bell Witch.

—MICHAEL GRISSOM,
Southern by the Grace of God

Ghosts, haunts, spirits, and apparitions have always
played a rich role in the folk tales of America. . . .

> At the head of this list stands the strange story of the
> Bell Witch of Adams, Tennessee, a continuing saga
> now nearly two centuries old.
>
> —*Quad-City* (IA) *Times,*
> October 24, 1980

An event transpires. How will it be remembered through time? John Bell died on December 24, 1820. Under ordinary circumstances, his death would hardly have caused a stir to those outside his immediate family; however, he was reportedly the only person to be killed by the Bell Witch. How exactly did this story evolve to reach the eyes and ears of countless people worldwide? A story is a "jigsaw puzzle" assembled from pieces of different sizes and origins. We cannot dispute that *something* happened at the Bell farm from 1817 to 1820 that caused various parts of this "puzzle" to come together in a certain way. This raises the question: how did the story evolve as each generation of storytellers interpreted the tale—perhaps differently? The focus of this chapter will be not only how the Bell Witch story survived at all, but also how it was propagated during the eighty years after its inception.

We have already considered the power of gossip and storytelling in a given culture. It is thereby extremely unlikely that the Bell family's neighbors did not gossip about what was allegedly taking place at the Bell house. In an era with few amusements, ignoring such a tantalizing series of events would have been difficult. By virtue of its entertainment value, the story would have spread like a virus from person to person. It is also reasonable to assume that storytellers repeated the tale and sometimes embellished the story to make it more enjoyable to hear. Guthrie, Kentucky, was just a few miles from Adams, Tennessee. Guthrie's oldest citizen in 1899 was "Father" John Kendall, who claimed that his recollections dated back to "the last war with England," referencing the War of 1812. He further reported, "I also remember going to the home of the celebrated 'Bell Witch' and hearing the older people talk of the mysterious performances."[1] Another person declared, "And in older times I have heard many weird tales as marvelous as the strange old story of the Bell Witch and some sensible people then seemed to believe them as true as the gospel."[2]

During the early 1800s, many people in the area moved to new regions in search of new opportunities. Often, these migrants moved west or south. Zadok Bell moved to Florida and Alabama. Joshua Gardner relocated to Weakley County in West Tennessee. Betsy Bell and her family moved to Yalobusha County, Mississippi, while Jesse Bell and other family members started a new home in Panola County, Mississippi.[3] My own family migrated from North Carolina to Robertson County, Tennessee, in the early 1800s. From there, some moved to Western Kentucky, Arkansas, Texas, and elsewhere. When people moved from Robertson County, they took their stories and superstitions with them.

Three additional factors, all relevant to the early nineteenth century, may have influenced Americans' views of supernatural events. Though they did not all impact Robertson County directly, it is likely that residents had a working knowledge of these happenings, which in turn shaped their perceptions. Earlier, we examined how a comet and earthquakes influenced how local citizens interpreted the Bell Witch story. We can then assume that a volcanic explosion would certainly help to shape their dogma as well. On April 10, 1815, the Mount Tambura volcano in the Dutch East Indies erupted—the largest explosion in hundreds of years— and created what became known as the "year without a summer." New England, eastern Canada, and parts of Western Europe were seriously affected, especially farming areas. Although Tennessee was not negatively impacted, the disaster was widely reported and no doubt added to locals' interpretation of "apocalyptic" conditions.[4]

We also cannot overlook the spiritualism movement, which very well may have opened many minds to the possibility of the supernatural. Spiritualism, or the belief that people could commune with the spirits of the dead and at times receive spiritual guidance, was a movement with European roots that emerged in the United States in the 1840s. The core of the movement was in the "Burned-Over District" of upstate New York, so-called from the numerous religious movements that had emerged from the region, including Millerism and Mormonism.[5] Vestiges of spiritualism remain today, with many people still seeking to communicate with spirits.[6]

Although the spiritualism movement was not especially prevalent in Middle Tennessee, there are some observable similarities between the otherworldly practice and the Bell Witch lore. A significant aspect of spiritualism was the belief that the spirits of the dead could communicate with the living through "spirit rapping." The Bell Witch story includes episodes in which the witch "rapped" and made other sounds. Often when attempting to communicate with the dead, spiritualists sought—usually through the guidance of a medium—advice about the future. According to the legend, the witch often predicted the future and prophesied about the Civil War, World War I, and World War II.[7]

Edgar Cayce further exemplified certain peoples' openness to the supernatural. Cayce, a Hopkinsville native who lived from 1877 until 1945, became known as the "sleeping prophet." People came to him for advice or to question him about wide-ranging subjects including health, war, reincarnation, and other queries about the future. Cayce would then fall asleep and, upon awakening, answer their questions. The proximity of Hopkinsville, Kentucky, to Adams, Tennessee, is no mere coincidence when considering the ideological impact of this "sleeping prophet."[8]

So far, we have discussed how local and global events contributed to an openness to supernatural events; but we are yet to explore how people beyond the region became acquainted with the story. One of the first print articles about the Bell Witch that may have reached a larger audience appeared in the *Saturday Evening Post*. In early 1856, an article entitled "The Tennessee Ghost" appeared in two separate newspapers. One was in the *Green Mountain* (VT) *Freeman* and the other was in the *New England Farmer* (Boston). They were the same article, and both were attributed to the *Saturday Evening Post*. Researchers, however, cannot agree if this *Post* article even existed. Regardless of the dubious origins of the original article, the Bell Witch pieces in the *Green Mountain Freeman* and the *New England Farmer* introduced new readers to the legend.[9]

A little over a decade later, a murder occurred in Robertson County that brought copious attention to the Bell Witch story. On September 9, 1868, Thomas Clinard, along with his accomplice, Richard Burgess, killed Charles Smith with two shots from a double-barreled shotgun. All three men were Robertson County residents. Both Clinard and Burgess were indicted for first-degree murder by the Robertson County Circuit Court during the October 1868 term. They testified under oath that they killed Smith in self-defense and that he had bragged about being a wizard who could cast spells using powers that he received from the Bell Witch. The trial was prolonged until March 1870. Ultimately, the jury declared both men "not guilty."[10] This murder and subsequent verdict evidence that belief in the Bell Witch was still prevalent in Robertson County, even fifty years after John Bell's death. The trial received newspaper coverage, appearing on the front page of the *Louisville Courier-Journal*, among others.[11] This attention helped keep the legend alive.

In 1880, a decade after Clinard and Burgess's murder trial, another reportedly supernatural event occurred in Springfield (the county seat of Robertson County), sparking renewed interest in the Bell Witch story. It took place in the home of a local physician John W. Nuckolls. According to the story, over the course of several days in April 1880, many people heard knocking sounds come from under the floor in one of the rooms in the Nuckolls's house. Though some people eventually came to believe that Mrs. Nuckolls most likely had attached an iron ball to a rubber belt under her clothes, the story was repeated in local newspapers along with the suggestion that perhaps the Bell Witch was involved.[12] The Bell Witch legend thus lived on.

Six years later, the Bell Witch story was brought to an even wider audience. In the early 1880s a Nashville-based publishing company headed by Westin A. Goodspeed published several state and county histories that became known as "Goodspeed Histories"; these works included history and biographies. In 1886, the company produced a history of seven Middle Tennessee counties, including Robertson. The study of Robertson County included a brief account of the Bell Witch legend. In the 1970s, nearly a full century later, the book was reprinted by two Middle Tennessee publishers.[13] The Goodspeed history of Robertson County introduced the story to a new audience and reminded readers of the staying power of superstition. As to an explanation for why the legend was included in the history, the author had this to say, "It is merely introduced as an example of superstition, strong in the minds of all but a few in those times, and not yet wholly extinct."[14]

Combined, migration and oral storytelling, cosmic and geological events, religion and spiritualism, and a wider awareness of the legend achieved through intermittent publications were all vital to the preservation and transmission of the Bell Witch legend from 1817 to 1894. All these together, however, were still not as important for the future of the story than the 1894 publication of M. V. Ingram's book, *Authenticated History of the Bell Witch*. The skeleton of the Bell Witch story had been constructed by 1894. Ingram put the meat on the bones of the legend.

Ingram was born in Guthrie, Kentucky, in 1832. As Guthrie was located only a few miles north of Adams, Ingram spent much of his life in "Bell

Witch territory." In the 1860s, Ingram worked as a coeditor of the *Robertson Register* newspaper in Springfield, Tennessee, just a few miles south of Adams. In 1869, he became the editor of the *Tobacco-Leaf* (which later became the *Leaf-Chronicle*) in Clarksville, Tennessee. The *Leaf-Chronicle* is still published today. Like Guthrie and Springfield, Clarksville is located only a few miles from Adams.[15] Ingram became a successful newspaper writer and editor. And, given that Ingram grew up and lived in an area in which he frequently heard Bell Witch stories, he recognized a good yarn when he heard it. Perhaps he realized early on that he might reap a financial reward by writing and publishing the first book about the Bell Witch legend.

He also received abundant support from the *Leaf-Chronicle*. Although he was no longer working for the newspaper when he published the book, he had strong ties with its higher-ups, especially its editor, W. P. Titus. From October 1893 until November 1894, the *Leaf-Chronicle* published over a dozen articles about the book, most of which were complimentary. For example, the June 6, 1894, article explained, "Mr. Ingram's Book, '*The Bell Witch*,' is interesting and is written in an easy style. It is also a strong argument, indirectly, in support of the theory of witchcraft."[16]

In the introduction to *Ghost Stories of Tennessee*, A. S. Mott wrote:

> What makes for a good ghost story? Having written my seventh paranormal book, I have concluded that a good ghost story requires at least two of the following elements:
>
> 1. A ghost or some other sort of supernatural creature
> 2. An intriguing back story explaining the origin of said ghost/ supernatural creature
> 3. A once-skeptical living person whose experience with the ghost/ supernatural creature has a profound effect on their life
> 4. The Civil War
> 5. A celebrity
> 6. A landmark

Of the above-listed elements, Ingram fulfilled elements one through three and five. (Four and six will be explored in later chapters.) Remarkably, Ingram met these markers more than one hundred years before Mott identified them. Arguably, the most compelling of these markers was the inclusion of a "celebrity." In the case of Ingram's Bell Witch book, the author outlined Andrew Jackson's own encounter with the witch.[17] Including Jackson in the story was an example what, over one hundred years later, Seth Godin coined the "purple cow" marketing concept and was a brilliant addition to the Bell Witch saga.[18] The concept of the purple cow is simple. While driving down the road, you see white, black, and spotted cows. Of course, you ignore them because you have seen such cows countless times. However, if you were one day to see a purple cow, you would stop and stare. You have never seen a purple cow before, so the cow now has your undivided attention.[19] The "purple cow" is a business and marketing concept that helps entrepreneurs set themselves and their company or product apart from their competitors. Purple cows can help a company win customers and convince them to buy things they normally might not have purchased. M. V. Ingram wrote a Bell Witch book in 1894. It is still in print today.

The following are just a few of the dozens of books and newspaper articles that repeat the Bell Witch/Jackson story:

Page Conan Doyle, "Jackson and "Famous" Bell Witch," *Louisville Courier-Journal,* January 27, 1925.

T. H. Alexander and Ben Bass, "The No. 1 Ghost Story," *Coronet,* July 1, 1937, 47 52.

"Andrew Jackson and the Bell Witch," *Montgomery* (AL) *Advertiser,* June 18, 1943.

"Andrew Jackson and the Bell Witch," in B. A. Botkin, ed. *A Treasury of Southern Folklore* (New York, Crown, 1949), 520–32.

"Bell Witch," *Nevada States Journal,* October 30, 1955

"The Bell Witch," in Susy Smith, *Prominent American Ghosts* (Cleveland, OH: World Publishing, 1967), 95–114.

"Ghosts I Can't Ignore," *Toronto* (Canada) *National Post,* March 27, 1971.

"Bewitched," *Santa Fe New Mexican* September 24, 1972.

Today Jackson's Nashville home, the Hermitage, is a historical site that stands as a monument to the seventh president. The Bell Witch has been incorporated into the on-site interpretation—not as truth, but as folklore. Today, the Hermitage has taken advantage of modern technology to keep the story alive; in 2019, the historic site produced an "All Hallows Eve" podcast called "Jackson and the Bell Witch."[20]

It must be said that the veracity of Jackson's "encounter" and Ingram's account is often questioned, but it makes for good entertainment, nonetheless. Ingram's work on the Bell Witch helped set the stage for the story's popularity well into the twentieth century—indeed, its influence on future writers and readers cannot be overstated. One thing is certain: Ingram knew how to craft a story. Other newspaper reporters did as well. The Bell Witch legend became a favorite topic for newspapers, especially at Halloween. The next chapter will consider the power of the press and the dispersion of the Bell Witch story.

five

THE POWER OF THE PRINTED WORD

Nowhere can be found ampler verification
of demonism than the columns of the
newspapers and periodical literature.

—*Louisville Courier-Journal*,
March 27, 1898

The Bell Witch of Robertson County has been
the subject of volumes of type.

—*Nashville Tennessean*,
October 30, 1932

Perhaps the most famous spine-tingler of the
1800s is the story of the "Bell Witch."

—*Selma* (AL) *Times Journal*,
May 9, 1971

Of all the eerie tales ever told, none is more
terrifying than the sinister story of the Bell Witch.
And every word of it is true.

—ALAN SPRAGGETT,
South Idaho Press, September 11, 1973

The Bell Witch haunting is notorious because
it may be best documented case of murder
by the supernatural in US history.

—*Hilo* (HI) *Tribune Herald,*
October 30, 2009

This is the West, sir, when the legend becomes fact,
print the legend.

—*The Man Who Shot Liberty Valance,* film

Since Ingram's Bell Witch book was published in 1894, and up until the last few decades, newspapers were the most influential sources of news, pop culture, stories, and folklore, and so forth. The two Bell family books, Harriet Miller's book, and magazines and journal articles were also important to the proliferation of the tale. Though the mediums differed, the written word was paramount. In the era before easy internet access, newspapers and magazines informed readers where they could purchase Bell Witch books. The February 1896 edition of the *Confederate Veteran Magazine* advertised that the Ingram book could be found at Setliff & Co., located at 511 Church Street in Nashville. Dozens of advertisements for the Bell Witch book appeared in Tennessee newspapers.[1]

Once the Ingram book was out of print, readers turned to newspapers for help finding copies. In 1930, a man wrote to the Clarksville *Leaf-Chronicle* seeking assistance. In 1955, a woman from Pennington Gap, Virginia, made the same request for help from the *Knoxville Journal.* The *Leaf-Chronicle* received numerous requests for help finding the Ingram book.[2] In 1961, Ingram's Bell Witch book was reprinted in a paperback edition. The *Nashville Tennessean* ran an article about the reprinted edition entitled "The Bell Witch is Making News in Nashville Again." In another article, the newspaper alerted its readers that, for $1.98, Zibart's Bookstore would promptly fill mail orders for the book.[3] The Clarksville *Leaf-Chronicle* kept its readers informed regarding where they could purchase the new edition.[4] No other book got the same special attention during this time.

While helping readers locate Ingram's book was important to the proliferation of the story, even more significantly, these newspapers passed on the story of the Bell Witch to future generations. From 1894 until the present, there have been thousands of Bell Witch newspaper and magazine articles. The following is merely a small sampling of these many publications, categorized by decade.

1890–1900

A few years prior to the publication of the Ingram book, these articles covered strange, perhaps witch-related events, in Adams: "A Rural Fake: A Mulhattanism from Adams Station, " *Louisville Courier-Journal,* February 3, 1890; and "A Weird Witch: More Tales of a Fishy Flavor from Adams Station, TN," February 21, 1890. Response to the 1894 publication of the Ingram book was immediate not only in Tennessee and Kentucky, but also around the country. The following headlines offer examples of this fascination:

"Famous Bell Witch of Tennessee, A Mystery that Baffled Even Old Hickory, Marvelous Manifestations Stronger than Spiritualism," *Cincinnati Enquirer,* July 14, 1894. (borrowed from the New York World)

"WITCHCRAFT IN THE SOUTHLAND, Surpasses Anything Found in the Annals of Salem, Story of the Famous Bell Witch and its Tragic Persecution of an Entire Family in Tennessee, 'Old Kate Batts' Awful Spell, and Some Other Marvelous Manifestations," *New Orleans Times-Picayune,* July 26, 1894.

"Witchcraft Down South, Betsy Bell Sees the Witch in the Woods, Story of the Famous Bell Witch of TN," *Minneapolis Star Tribune,* July 15, 1894.

"Witchcraft Down South," The *Larned* (KS) *Eagle-Optic,* August 3, 1894.

"Story of Witchcraft: History of the Famous Bell Witch," *Ohio County* (KY) *News,* July 25, 1894.

"History of the Bell Witch," *Nashville Banner,* June 9, 1894.

The Clarksville *Tobacco-Leaf Chronicle* was the most ardent reporter of both the Ingram book and the Bell Witch legend. Between 1894 and 1900, the newspaper published over thirty articles about the book and its story. In a July 30, 1894, article the newspaper reported that "since the publication of the book many are afraid to venture out alone after dark." This newspaper's support of the book can most likely be attributed to Ingram's close ties to the news outlet.

However, the newspaper's endorsement of the story did bring, some criticism from local readers. The following article appeared in the June 15, 1894, issue of the paper: "DENOUNCED THE BOOK, Rev. J. C. Chenault of St. Bethlehem Fires Into the Bell Witch." The preacher declared that after the publication of the book "the county was running wild" and the book "is not worth reading." A reader of the *Hopkinsville Kentuckian* from Casky, Kentucky, seemed to agree when he wrote, "reading 'The Bell Witch' is quite the custom here now and the whole community is full of witches, two-headed dogs and graveyard rabbits after dark."[5] By 1896, newspaper coverage of the Bell Witch story had slowed, but had not stopped altogether. Some examples of this later attention include a *Nashville Banner* article entitled "Old Times in Robertson! Some Remarkable and Amusing Capers of the Celebrated 'Bell Witch'," August 26, 1896, and a *Louisville Courier-Journal* article, "The Strange Survival of the Demon Idea," March 27, 1898.

1900–1910

By 1900, the excitement stirred by Ingram's book had subsided, but not disappeared. In that same year, the *Clarksville Tobacco-Leaf Chronicle* published a whimsical piece that reported, "Evidently Ezekiel has taken to drinking nothing stronger than river water and reading nothing stronger than The Bell Witch . . . his dreams have improved."[6] Also that year a review of the Bell Witch Story was included in the American Historical Magazine published in Nashville.[7] Renewed interest in the story peaked once again in 1903. In one popular retelling of the legend, it was reputed that Kate would return to Adams sometime in the future. Versions of the legend predicted different years for her return, but it was often speculated that the witch would return in 1903, the centennial of the Bell family's arrival in Robertson County.[8] This version of the story sparked several newspaper articles including:

"Will Tennessee's Terrible 'Bell Witch' Keep Its Promise," *Cincinnati Enquirer*, May 10, 1903.

"Newspaper Pipe Dream, Nobody in Robertson County Excited
   About the Bell Witch," *Nashville American*, August 30, 1903.
"Nobody in Robertson County Excited About the Bell Witch,"
   Clarksville Leaf-Chronicle, August 31, 1903.
"Bell Witch Due to Arrive Again, According to Promise," *Hopkinsville
   Kentuckian*, September 1, 1903.
"The Bell Witch: History of the Greatest Mystery in Tennessee,"
   Paducah News-Democrat, September 6, 1903.

The *Hopkinsville Kentuckian* put an end to the "return" craze when it
republished an article from the *Springfield Herald*, reporting that, "The
Bell Witch must have gotten her dates mixed up, August has come and
gone and yet we have heard nothing of her promised return."[9] Several
newspapers during the decade had columns to answer questions from
readers. Some of the requests were for information about the Bell Witch.
Some newspapers issued responses, including:

Henry M. Wiltse, "The Bell Witch Mystery," *Chattanooga* (TN) *News*,
   August 4, 1904.
A. I. Baird, "Witches, Men, and Things, *Nashville Banner*, May 23,
   1905.
"Purely Personal" column, *Chattanooga Daily Times*, June 12, 1906.
"Banner's Query Box," *Nashville Banner*, September 1, 1907.

1910–1930

From 1910–1930, newspapers showed subdued interest in the Bell Witch
story. Most of the stories that were published during this time were from
Tennessee and Kentucky newspapers. The legend had not yet developed
a widespread audience despite national newspaper coverage for Ingram's
book in the 1890s. This quickly changed in the 1930s, however, with yet
another promise that the witch would return to Adams. Even so, articles
during this twenty-year period stoked interest in the Bell Witch folklore.
Examples included:

Lucy S. V. King, "Strange Old Story of the Bell Witch," *Nashville
   American*, June 26, 1910.
A. Layman, "Mysteries of Olden Times, Bell's Witch Mystery," *Nash-
   ville Banner*, August 22, 1914.

"Robertson, Tennessee County, Home of the Bell Witch of Uncanny Fame," *Knoxville Journal and Tribune*, November 8, 1923.

Newspapers continued to receive requests from readers for more information about the witch, and some devoted special sections to answering such questions. The *Nashville Banner* called its column the "Banners Query Book," while the *Chattanooga News*'s was called "Dropped Stitches." The *Clarksville Leaf-Chronicle* received a request from "L.D.C." in Lawrence, Kansas for information on the Bell Witch to be used in a thesis.[10] Further, the story received the attention it had been sorely lacking when *McClure's Magazine* published an article by Irvin S. Cobb on the Bell Witch. Cobb was a well-known writer and McClure's had a nationwide audience, which made for a winning combination. A *Chattanooga Daily Times* article declared that Cobb had made the story a "classic tale."[11]

1930–1940

The nature of the printed word changed dramatically in the 1930s, in part due to an increased literacy rate. Additionally, some syndicates owned several newspapers, which made it easier to share stories from one part of the country to another. Largely thanks to newspapers, the Bell Witch story became known nationwide. And, a new Bell Witch book was published.[12]

Occasionally during the early 1930s, newspaper articles appeared concerning the legend, most of which originated in Tennessee and Kentucky papers.[13] A *Nashville Tennessean* article claimed, "The Bell Witch had a South-wide fame and attracted investigations from foreign countries.[14] This "South-wide fame" would soon develop into national renown, with the "return of the Bell Witch." In 1935, a brief flurry of articles pertained to the anticipated 1935 return of the witch. The *Des Moines Register* (IA) published a nearly one-half page article entitled "Famed Ghost Back in '35 After 107 Years Absence; Miraculous Feats of 'Bell Witch' Stirred Nation Century Ago; President Andrew Jackson Saw It Perform."[15]

The most influential story was the "1937 return." The idea that the witch would return in 1937 can be traced to an article in the *Nashville Tennessean*, in which journalist T. H. Alexander wrote a syndicated column called "I Reckon So." He had often used this same column for Bell Witch stories. On January 3, 1937, he wrote that the poltergeist was "practically certain to return to earth in this good year 1937." This prediction was based on information he and Ben Bass had uncovered during research for a long article on the Witch. Other articles suggested this future event as well.[16]

From these starting points, the return story expanded throughout the United States. Numerous articles from dozens of newspapers spread the story from the East Coast to the West Coast and states between. The story spread due in no small part to the syndication of newspapers and the tendency for newspapers to "copy" stories from each other. For example, Robert Talley's article "America's No. 1 Ghost Breaks a Date Made 110 Years Ago" appeared in the *Memphis Commercial Appeal* on October 31, 1937; then, on December 19, 1937, the same story was printed in the *Ogden Standard-Examiner* (UT), the *Spokane Spokesman-Review* (WA), the *Montana Standard,* and the *Arizona Republic.* On March 6, 1938, that very article could be read in the *Hartford Courant* (CT). Many of the dozens of identical articles contained pictures and some filled one-half a page or more. Although the Bell Witch did not return in spirit, she did arrive in print and in the imaginations of readers.

1940–1960

The decade began with the publication of *God Bless the Devil! Liars' Bench Tales* by writers from the Tennessee Writers' Project. The book included a tale called "The Hag of Red River" about the Bell Witch.[17] In the same year, the *Memphis Commercial Appeal* featured an article titled "Far Famed Bell Witch, Still Lives in Legend after 113 Years."[18] In 1948, the *Nashville Tennessean Magazine* published "The Rowdy Witch." According to the magazine, its decision to do so was based upon a lingering inquiry; as the magazine explained: "Why don't you do a story on the Bell Witch is a question which has confronted the magazine ever since it was established nearly three years ago."[19] Other newspaper stories pertaining to witches were also produced during this decade, especially from Tennessee and Alabama. An article called "The Mystery of the Bell Witch" appeared in newspapers in Alabama, Iowa, Wyoming, and Nevada. A variety of other Bell Witch stories were published in newspapers in California, Alabama, New York, Vermont, Iowa, and Kentucky and Tennessee.

1960–1970

Among the traditional stories about the myth, three stories are especially notable. The January 23, 1960, edition of the *Clarksville Leaf-Chronicle* published a letter to the editor; a reader wanted to know if a recent siren heard in the city was a warning of the return of the Bell Witch. In a *Detroit Free Press* article, a woman claimed that she was "a direct descendant of the famous Southern 'witch' called the Bell Witch of Tennessee and had many experiences in the realm of the supernatural." She also claimed that, with the help of a psychic, she was able to "break the violent ties between her and her family curse."[20]

The *Lincoln* (NE) *Journal Star* published a review of Susy Smith's book *Prominent American Ghosts*. The reviewer wrote, "This book is something else. Just the thing to curl up with at 3 a.m. on a cold, windy night and figure how not to get the shivers. Especially when reading 'The Bell Witch.'"[21] In other sources, Andrew Tackaberry published a book about supernatural events that included a chapter on the Bell Witch, and Peggy Robbins wrote a magazine article called "Exploring the Unknown about the Witch Story."[22]

1970–2000

Over the last fifty years, print newspapers and magazines have played a less important role in American culture. This decline began in earlier decades but has increased more rapidly over the last half century. Print media competes with radio, television, telephones, and the internet. Even so, print media has remained a major source of information for many people. From 1970 to 2000, newspaper articles about the Bell Witch appeared in print in Tennessee, Alabama, North Carolina, Iowa, Mississippi, Wisconsin, and Vancouver, Canada. Three articles were of special interest. In 1972, Hugh Walker, who worked for the *Nashville Tennessean*, wrote a piece on the Bell Witch. Walker asked Charles Willet, who was from Robertson County and a Bell descendant, if the Bell Witch was real. Willet looked over his glasses and answered, "The Bell Witch was as real as any other witch."[23]

In a February 1973 article, Christopher Dafoe, a Canadian poet and author with a column in the *Vancouver Sun* (British Columbia), reviewed books about spirits, including those on what he called the "celebrated

Bell Witch."[24] The *Wisconsin Rapids Daily Tribune* printed an article about "haunts and apparitions," reporting, "At the head of the list stands the strange story of the Bell Witch of Adams, Tennessee."[25] In addition to newspaper articles, several books were published concerning supernatural events; most of them featured Bell Witch stories. In her book, Natalie Osborne-Thomason declared, "The story of the Bell Witch has gone down in history as possibly one of the most malevolent poltergeist hauntings ever recorded."[26]

2000–2020

As this narrative approached the present, fewer Bell Witch newspaper articles appeared, as the internet had become a major source of information. Still, several articles saw publication. A reader of the *Sacramento* (CA) *Bee* sent the paper a note asking if a ghost had ever killed someone. The *Bee* responded that the best documented case was John Bell and the Bell Witch.[27] In a column about Halloween stories, a writer for the *Vancouver Canada Sun* referred to the Bell Witch as "truly a poltergeist from hell."[28] The *Danville Advocate-Messenger* (KY) published a Halloween article titled "Revisiting the Murderous Bell Witch."[29] A writer for an Alabama paper explained that, "The best known of the 'family' ghost stories is the haunting of John Bell's house near Adams, Tennessee by a poltergeist known as the Bell Witch."[30] On a lighter note, the Williamson County, Tennessee Public Library System started a R.E.A.D.S (Regional E-book and Audiobook Downloadable Systems) program, through which students could access more than two thousand audio and e-books. The most requested items were books about the Bell Witch.[31] Compilations of supernatural stories also feature the Bell Witch legend.[32] Newspapers proved that, over time, the Witch folklore found readers throughout the United States and even in Canada. In recent times, it would be up to other media outlets to spread the story worldwide.

This legend of bigfoot has endured in the United States and Canada since the early 1800s and centers around humanlike creatures that might be missing links between Homo sapiens and apelike creatures.

Every year Point Pleasant holds a Mothman festival in celebration of the popular legend.

The story of the "Little Green Men" of Kelly, Kentucky,
while unsubstantiated, remains a popular tale.

Portrait of John Bell Jr.

JOHN BELL
1750 —— 1820

ORIGINAL TOMBSTONE
DISAPPEARED ABOUT 1951
THIS MARKER PLACED 1957
HIS WIFE
LUCY WILLIAMS BELL

John Bell's grave marker. Photo by Jerrod Johnson.

The Infamous Bell Witch of Tennessee by Charles Edwin Price
was originally published in 1994.

AUTHENTICATED HISTORY

OF THE

BELL WITCH

And Other Stories of the World's Greatest Unexplained Phenomenon.

— BY —

M. V. INGRAM.

The Authenticated History of the Bell Witch and Other Stories of the World's Greatest Unexplained Phenomenon by M. V. Ingram was originally published in 1894 and was the first of dozens of Bell Witch books.

OXFORD
··· AMERICAN ···

ISSUE #35 SEPTEMBER / OCTOBER 2000 $5.95   THE SOUTHERN MAGAZINE OF GOOD WRITING

A Haunting in Tennessee
William Gay Pursues the Bell Witch

**UFOS AND ALIENS
IN ARKANSAS**
by Matthew Teague

**NEW ORLEANS'
FORGOTTEN
RACE RIOT**
by Annie Wedekind

**RESCUING THE
RED WOLVES OF
NORTH CAROLINA**
by Jan DeBlieu

**CALENDAR GIRL:
A STORY OF LOVE
AND RAGE**
by James Carlos Blake

display until November 2000

A Painted House
by John Grisham
(Part 5)

$3.95 (Canada $7.95)

Due to newspaper articles and magazine stories,
the story of the Bell Witch spread internationally.

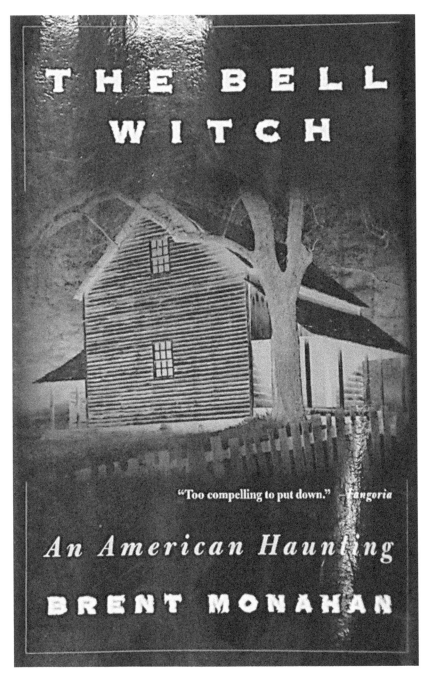

"Too compelling to put down." —*Fangoria*

An American Haunting

BRENT MONAHAN

The Bell Witch, An American Haunting by Brent Monahan
was originally published in 1997.

Carney and Bob Bell, descendants of John Bell,
at the grave of Joel Bell, son of John Bell.

Timothy Henson holding copies of the three
Bell Witch books. Photo by Jerrod Johnson.

THE NASHVILLE THEATRE ACADEMY   presents
                                          a true story

OUR FAMILY TROUBLE:
THE LEGEND OF THE BELL WITCH

Dramatized by Audrey Campbell
with technical assistance by
Ken Lambert and Thomas Kartak

OCTOBER 25 through DECEMBER 17

Directed by	Thomas Kartak
Set Design by	Geoffrey Sedgwick & Thomas Kartak
Costume Design by	Estelle Worrell
Technical Direction by	Geoffrey Sedgwick
Special Effects by	Don Elwell
Lighting Design by	Geoffrey Sedgwick
Stage Management by	Linda McCulloch
Music & Sound by	Steve Wheaton
Recording Engineering	by Neil Wright
Projections by	Geoffrey Sedgwick
Program Cover and Poster Art by	David Wright of Graystone Gallery
Lobby Display by	Rose Pickel

All crews headed and staffed by the Volunteer Membership of the
Nashville Children's Theatre Association

THE CAST

JOHN BELL . . . . .T. J. Jochim

LUCE BELL . . . . Elizabeth Ann Dyrcz

BETSY BELL . . . . Carol Ann Mansell

JOHNNY BELL . . . . Don Elwell

RICHARD BELL . . . . J. R. Wears

JOSHUA GARDNER . . . . Ken Lambert

SUGG FORT. . . . . Paul Klapper

RICHARD POWELL . . . . Ken Thompson

JOE EDWARDS . . . . Robert McCrary

DR. MIZE . . . . Morris Brown

KATE BATTS . . . . Phebe Day

JAMES GUNN . . . . Dan Brown

THE SPIRITUAL UNITY

BLACKDOG. . . . . Ruth Sweet

MATHEMATICS . . . . Cameille Reagon

CYPOCRYPHY . . . . Trish Thompson

JERUSALEM . . . . Michael Haworth

Our Family Trouble: The Legend of the Bell Witch became well known
and was reviewed by newspapers across the country.

Mercyful Fate album cover, 1994. In 1993 Mercyful Fate released "The Bell Witch." The opening lyrics proclaimed, "Back in Tennessee, I saw a family haunted by an entity. It was a tragedy in another century."

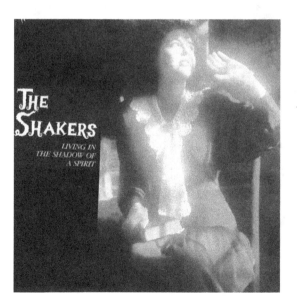

In 1986 The Shakers formed in Nashville with plans to write songs based on the famous Tennessee legend. They subsequently became one of Music City's most popular rock bands.

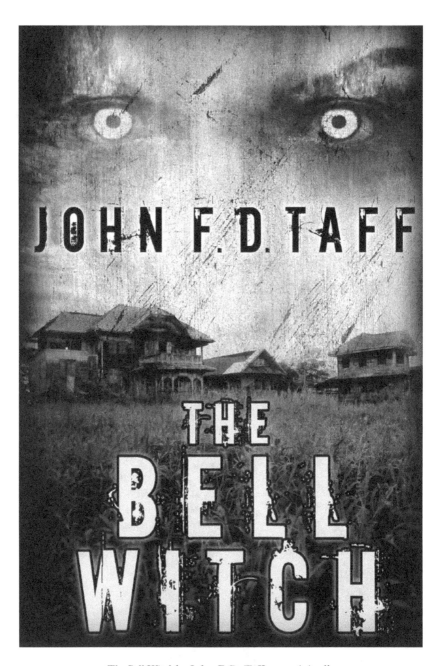

The Bell Witch by John F. D. Taff was originally
published in 2013.

"Bell Witch Haunting" movie poster, 2013.
This was one of several Bell Witch movies.

Over time, the Bell Witch became attached to items that had no connection to the legend or folklore. Photo courtesy of Darin Richardson and Kevin Mead.

Bell Witch Cave, Adams, Tennessee.

Many festivals and events have capitalized on the supernatural fame of Adams, Tennessee. Photo by Jerrod Johnson.

Sign on US 41 in Adams, Tennessee. Even President Andrew Jackson was said to have experienced "Old Kate's" mysterious powers firsthand.

Another sign on US 41 in Adams, Tennessee. The Bell Witch cave has become a major tourist attraction in the small town of Adams. Photo by Jerrod Johnson.

Bell Witch Forge attraction.

The legend of the Bell Witch has inspired many events, including
the 2012 Bluegrass Competition. Photo by Jerrod Johnson.

A poster for the 2012 Old-Time & Bluegrass Contest.

Musical events have helped attract tourists to the area.
Photo by Jerrod Johnson.

David Alford, "SPIRIT" playwright, and Jenny Littleton, the "voice" of the Bell Witch in "SPIRIT" for twelve years. Photo courtesy of Sam Ramsey, 2006.

Cast of the first production of "SPIRIT" in Adams, 2002.
Courtesy of the City of Adams Museum and Archives.
Photo of original print by Jerrod Johnson.

"SPIRIT" cast photo, 2017.

Audience at a "SPIRIT" performance, 2019. Photo by Katie Veglio.

SIX

ACADEMICS, FOLKLORISTS, AND OTHER ENTITIES FALL UNDER THE SPELL

"The Case of the Bell Witch" reads like
a mystery novel.

—NANDOR FODOR,
The Haunted Mind

Belief in ghosts, witches and demons may be as old as
the human capacity to symbolize.

—CHARLES EDWIN PRICE,
Haunts, Witches, and Boogers

Most people are aware that Tennessee
is rich in folklore.

—ELEANOR E. GOEHRING,
Tennessee Folk Culture

The legend of the Bell Witch recounts the misfortunes
of a family named Bell who moved from North
Carolina to the midlands of Tennessee in the
early 1800s and then, in one branch, to northern
Mississippi, about forty years later.

—ARTHUR PALMER HUDSON AND
PETE KYLE MCCARTER,
The Bell Witch of Tennessee and Mississippi

The three best known folk tales are Paul Bunyan,
the Jack Tales, and Tennessee's Bell Witch

—*Chattanooga Daily Times,*
Nov. 9, 1947

The purpose of Chapter 5 was not to provide an exhaustive list of all the newspaper and magazine articles concerning the Bell Witch legend, but rather to present enough examples to let the reader know how important print media, especially newspapers, have been to the story's dissemination. The focus of this chapter will be the roles played by academics, folklorists, and other entities in the continued spread of the tale. A rewarding place to start a study of the publications about the Bell Witch in folklore is Eleanor E. Goehring's *Tennessee Folk Culture: An Annotated Bibliography.* Goehring's book could also be used to understand the legend's place in the larger arena of folklore studies.[1]

One of the first mentions of the Bell Witch in a folklore journal is in Tom Peete Cross's article in 1909, "Folklore from the Southern States."[2] One of the most recognized folklore articles was Arthur Palmer Hudson and Pete Kyle McCarter's piece, "The Bell Witch of Tennessee and Mississippi: A Folk Legend."[3] Prior to publishing the article, the authors gave a series of lectures at the University of North Carolina, including a talk to the Philological Club there.[4] A shorter version of their article appeared in a Reader's Digest book in 1978.[5]

Harry A. Hargrave grew up close to the Bell farm and later became an English professor at North Carolina State University. He remembered hearing the Bell Witch stories and reported that "my mother read me Charles Bailey Bell's account, chapter by chapter as I ate my daily lunches." He also recounted that he wrote a folklore article about the legend with "some hope of bringing into order the events that had often been recorded."[6]

In addition to written stories, lectures about the Bell Witch legend were popular on college campuses. In 1934, the Study Club of the Alumnae Chapter of the Alpha Omicron Pi Sorority met at its chapter house to hear Dr. Bailey Bell speak about his book, *The Mysterious Spirit.*[7] In 1947, the Vanderbilt University Women's Club met at Alumni Hall to hear Mrs. Norman E. Jackson's presentation, "The Legend of the Bell Witch."[8] In 2006, Tennessee Tech University professor Paula Hinton taught a class

entitled "Ghosts, Myths, and Legends in American History," which included a block on the Bell Witch.[9] In 2011, Nashville's Lipscomb University's "Lifelong Learning Program" included a class on the Bell Witch of
Adams.[10] In 2016, Dr. Amy Laurel Fluker delivered a lecture on "The Bell
Witch of Mississippi" at the University of Mississippi."[11]

The establishment of folklore programs at several American universities further facilitated the spread of the Bell Witch legend and other
tales. One of the most advantageous avenues for the spread of the Bell
Witch story began in 1970 at Western Kentucky University. The institution
launched a MA degree program in folk studies under the guidance of
Lynwood Montell.[12] Because the university was approximately fifty miles
from Adams, many of the folklore students were afforded the opportunity
to conduct extended studies of the Bell Witch legend and interviewed
many local citizens about the legend. The interviews and student papers
are archived in the university's Folklife Archives in the Special Collections
Library. Indiana University also developed a folklore department in 1962.
One of the most important projects that the university undertook was the
publication of two books on folklore motifs, or similar stories that appear
over time and space in various folklore legends.[13] At Western Kentucky
University, Lynwood Montell had his students compare the Bell Witch
stories to motifs in the Thompson and Baughman books. Students found
numerous connections between the Bell Witch stories and general motifs,
including buried treasures, a lost tooth, attempts to burn a witch, nuts
and fruit falling onto people from the rafters and buildings, supernatural
poisoning, the presence of a black dog, and drinking songs.[14] One of the
best-known similarities, however, is the "mirror story" discussed in Chapter
3. This version has much in common with the infamous "Bloody Mary"
mirror folklore legend.[15] We have also considered the "rock superstition,"
whereby if you took a rock from the Bell Witch cave, she would "get" you,
which is similar to the very old "Big Toe" story. Simply put, if you stole the
"big toe," its owner would find you and hurt you. There are many variations of the tale.[16]

Nandor Fodor, an associate of Sigmund Freud, introduced the Bell
Witch story to a new field of academia. He was born in Hungary and received a doctorate in law before moving to New York and then to England,
working as a journalist. In the 1930s and 1940s, he turned his attention
to paranormal phenomena using a psychoanalytical point of view. In his
research on poltergeists and other paranormal experiences, he became

interested in the Bell Witch story and applied his beliefs to the legend. Fodor's work introduced the Bell Witch saga to a new group of readers and thinkers.[17] His writings also influenced other writers to apply psychoanalysis to their studies of the Bell Witch phenomena.[18]

Fodor's work was significant beyond the field of psychoanalysis. Newspapers published reviews of his book, including a review of *Haunted People* in the *Hartford Courant* (CT), December 30, 1951, and Joseph Henry Jackson's, "Bookman's Notebook: Naughty Ghosts," *Los Angeles Times*, January 15, 1952. In Barbara Michaels's novel *Other Worlds*, Fodor, Harry Houdini, and Sir Arthur Conan Doyle are in a smoke-filled room trying to decipher the Bell Witch phenomena.[19] Fodor's ideas also influenced the novel *The Bell Witch: An American Haunting* and the film *An American Haunting*.[20]

The Bell Witch legend became so well-known that other states have tried to claim the story for themselves. Though some claims were dubious, the states with the strongest demonstrable ties were North Carolina and Mississippi. An account of the North Carolina version of the Bell Witch story can be found in Pat Fitzhugh's *The Bell Witch: The Full Account*.[21] Gilbert E. Govan's article "Roaming the Realm of Books" tied the story to North Carolina folklore.[22] Albeit briefly, the Bell Witch of North Carolina was featured in *Playboy Magazine*.[23]

Mississippi also claimed the Bell Witch story for itself. Members of the Bell family moved to Panola and Yalobusha counties in the state. The story traveled with them, of course, along with other Tennesseans who relocated to Mississippi. Articles by Hudson and McCarter posit that the Bell Witch legend has roots in both Mississippi and Tennessee. The *Charleston Democratic-Herald* (MS) published a small book, *The Bell Witch*, which it offered for sale in over a dozen advertisements from July 22, 1897, to September 30, 1898. These ads occasionally ran on the front page of the newspaper. An article on August 12, 1897 stated that the book could be purchased for twenty-five cents at the newspaper office. A March 31, 1898, article reported that the book could be purchased for fifty-two cents, or was "free for every new subscriber or payment of delinquent back dues." In a March 20, 1986, article in the *Clarke County Tribune* (MS), the writer declared that the Bell Witch was "the most famous ghost in Mississippi."[24]

Kentucky not only shares a border with Tennessee, but Todd and Logan counties in Kentucky are close to Robertson County and Adams. Joe Creason wrote a column for the *Louisville Courier-Journal* from the

1950s to the 1970s. His column repeatedly included articles about the Bell Witch and the story's link to Kentucky. In a March 1, 1957, piece, he wrote "Spells, Hexes, Broomsticks . . . So What Did Salem Have that Kentucky Didn't?" In its October 30, 1968, edition, the *Madisonville Messenger* (KY) reprinted a Creason article from the *Courier-Journal* entitled "Kentucky's Famous Witch from Todd County Kentucky." An October 29, 2010, article in the *Russellville News-Democrat* (KY) *and Leader* continued the tradition.[25]

Alabama residents, much like Tennesseans, did not always embrace the legend of the Bell Witch. The following articles ran in Alabama newspapers in early 1912:

> "Bell Witch Frightens Blackburn Beat People," *Birmingham News*, February 24, 1912.
>
> "Bell Witch with Terrifying Scream Abroad in Lauderdale County," *Montgomery Advertiser*, February 25, 1912.
>
> "Bell Witch Frightens Blackbeat People," *Florence Herald*, March 3, 1912.
>
> Reports of Screams and Stranger Looking Animals," *Leighton News*, March 8, 1912.

Bill Rollow was trying to understand why his local baseball team was losing games. He wrote, "I wonder if the Bell Witch who haunted my house more than a hundred years ago hasn't come back and put grease on their throwing hands, lead in their gloves, and bad luck in their bats."[26] Illinois and Nova Scotia were not immune to blaming the supernatural for unfortunate circumstances. An October 1, 1949, article in the *Nashville Banner* about strange events in Illinois tied the occurrences to Robertson County to the Bell Witch. The article covered a half page and contained pictures of John Bell and the Bell Witch cave.[27]

Decades earlier, the *Banner* had printed an article about Nova Scotia, Canada, that drew parallels between local happenings and the Bell Witch: "They have a big ghost scare somewhere around Caledonia Mills, Nova Scotia and Dr. Walter Franklin Prince, a New York Scientist is now on the ground to prosecute an investigation. All this brings up reminiscences of the famous Bell Witch that created great excitement in Robertson County, Tennessee, many years ago."[28] Each of these areas experienced unexplained occurrences that were often blamed on the supernatural. In each case, a revived memory of the Bell Witch further propagated the legend. Such explanations were also seen in the federal government and certain Tennessee state institutions. In 1939, a federal government publication included a brief history of the Bell Witch legend and a reprint of the Bell Witch article from *Goodspeed History of Tennessee.*[29]

Tennesseans quickly realized that the Bell Witch story was good for tourism. When *USA Today* published a sixteen-page tabloid to celebrate "Tennessee Homecoming '86," it included an article on the Bell Witch.[30] In 1999, the Tennessee State Museum hosted a ghost story festival at the museum called "The Haunted Mansion." The festival included the story of the "infamous Bell Witch." "The Haunted Mansion" became a regular part of the museum's annual Halloween celebration.[31] The state park system also recognized the story's draw. In the last few years, Port Royal State Park, located close to Adams, has started conducting annual "Port Royal by Lantern" tours that feature Bell Witch tales. In 2019, the Bicentennial Capital Mall State Park in Nashville hosted a Tennessee Timeline celebration called "Stories and Sounds from Tennessee: From Bell Witch to Boycotts."[32] In 1998, the Tennessee Historical Society published *The Tennessee Encyclopedia of History and Culture,* which included an article written by William T. Turner called "Bell Witch."[33] In short, academics, folklorists, and government agencies have done much to disperse the Bell Witch story. The next chapter will explore the relationship between live performances, such as storytelling, ballets, and theater, and the continued dissemination of the legend.

seven

THE BELL WITCH LIVE

The power of the story has always been important
for humanity . . . and I think the interest in hearing
them told well stems from a desire for art that's
not mediated by electronic means . . . people are
hungry for direct experience.

—JOHN GENTILE,
Kennesaw State University,
Atlanta Constitution, October 24, 2002

I . . . used to swap Bell Witch stories
in my grandpa's coal bin.

—"MYSTERY MAN,"
Hartford Courant, (CT) June 27, 1988

My grandmother Mary Kathleen Self is responsible
for telling me this story when I was little and for
keeping it alive as I grew.

—MELISSA SANDERS-SELF,
All that Lives

I am truly nostalgic for a place in Cedar Hill (TN)—
the home of my grandmother's family.
We visited there often, sitting on the side porch
during the summertime while Bell Witch

stories were told or running in the yard
to catch lightning bugs.

—CHARLOTTE REEDY,
Robertson County Times, December 27, 2017

In the foreword of her Bell Witch novel, Melissa Sanders-Self proclaims, "I would like to thank all the people of Adams and Robertson County, Tennessee, those with us and those no longer present, who kept the tale of the Bell Witch alive, passing it down over nearly two hundred years. All those people unknown to me made this book possible."[1] She was right; local storytellers *did* keep the story alive. While the mediums and methodology have varied, storytelling has been proven paramount to the story's endurance and a continued belief in the power of the tale.

Each generation retells the old stories—adding an occasional embellishment or new tale. By doing so, local storytellers keep the story alive not only regionally but also in other parts of the country. As the *Asbury Park Press* (NJ) reported in an October 27, 1985, article, "Even in an age where superstition is met with skepticism, the folks around Adams can weave some mighty convincing tales of more recent encounters with the Bell Witch." The fact that newspapers continued to report on storytelling from the town of Adams and Robertson County kept the story relevant and—more importantly—contemporary.[2]

Over the last few decades, several Middle Tennessee and Southern Kentucky storytellers have entertained audiences of varied demographics. One of the most popular storytellers from the 1960s to the 1980s was W. M. "Bims" Eden. owned part of the Bell farm, including the Bell Witch cave. He was "theatrical" in his storytelling style, especially when relating his personal experiences with the witch. He was also a favorite of writers seeking information about the stories.[3] William Turner from Hopkinsville, Kentucky, was also a prolific Bell Witch storyteller. He taught history at Christian County High School for seven years, then at Hopkinsville Community College for thirty-two years, and served as the Hopkinsville City and Christian County historian. He told Bell Witch stories over one hundred times in Tennessee, Kentucky, Illinois, Indiana, and Ohio, and continues to recount these tales today. One of my daughter Suzanne's favorite memories is listening to William Turner tell Bell Witch stories on our own front porch.[4]

Also important in keeping the story alive over the last few decades are Carney and Bob Bell, Gene Davidson, and William "Bo" Adams. Carney and Bob Bell are descendants of John Bell. Gene Davidson is from Adams and served on behalf of Robertson County in the Tennessee House of Representatives from 1974 until 2006.[5] Bo Adams is a Robertson County historian who freely shared his extensive knowledge with me about the Bell Witch legend. Three other local Bell Witch storytellers—Dewey Edwards, Pat Fitzhugh, and Timothy R. Henson—have also written books, thus perpetuating the story.[6]

Though locals have made a strong showing in recounting the area's folklore, not all Bell Witch storytellers have been from Adams.[7] Jackie Torrence, also known as "America's favorite storyteller" for her stories about Black and Southern folk cultures, became one of the most prominent and popular Bell Witch storytellers in the country.[8]

Listening to stories from the legend became favorite events at women's book clubs, birthday parties, Boy Scout outings around campfires, language arts classes, and any gathering that lent itself to the opportunity to recount the tale. In Mississippi, the Committee for the Humanities funded a grant "to support the revival of storytelling, especially the Bell Witch."[9] In this way, storytellers kept the legend alive—sometimes speaking one on one and sometimes in front of dozens, or even hundreds, of people. Storytellers, however, are not the only live performers to circulate the account: the folklore also inspired a cantata, ballets, and numerous stage plays.

Charles Faulkner Bryan was born in McMinnville, Tennessee, in 1911. After attending Tennessee Polytechnic Institute and Peabody College, he studied music at Yale on a Guggenheim Fellowship. While there, he wrote *The Bell Witch Cantata*. His setting for the story was in North Carolina, where the Bells lived before coming to Robertson County in the early 1800s. The cantata opened to great acclaim at Carnegie Hall in New York City in 1947. Robert Shaw conducted the Julliard Chorus and Orchestra, which accompanied the cantata. The Bryan Collection can be found at Vanderbilt University's Jean and Alexander Heard Library, Special Collections.[10] Ultimately, the cantata introduced the Bell Witch to a new audience in New York City and beyond. On March 30, 1948, the performance had its Nashville premier. William Strickland conducted the Nashville Choral Society and the Nashville Symphony. Over the next several decades, *The Bell Witch Cantata* was produced either in whole or in part across the country. One performance was even held at California's Occidental College.[11] This version of the story revolves around a curse put on John Bell after he killed his farm overseer. The curse culminates when the witch kills Bell's daughter, Nancy. Of course, in the Adams version of the legend, Betsy is the daughter.

The Bell Witch story has been presented on stage through dance as well. In 1961, the Modern Dance Workshop and the Nashville Ballet Society sponsored a ballet performance of *Joy Zibart's brilliant Bell Witch Dance*.[12] The artistic relationship between ballet and the Bell Witch legend reached its pinnacle in the first decade of the 2000s with *The Bell Witch Ballet*, choreographed and composed by Ann Marie DeAngelo and Conni Ellisor. An early version of the ballet-in-progress was presented by the Nashville Ballet in collaboration with the Nashville Chamber Orchestra as the season opener in October 2001.[13] The ballet also opened the 2003 Nashville Ballet season with a focus on three prevailing themes from the legend: the witch as a disturbing force, the witch's interference in the proposed marriage of Betsy Bell and Joshua Gardner, and the death of John Bell. The ballet was reviewed by several newspapers around the country, including Associated Press affiliates,[14] received worldwide attention when it was nominated for the prestigious Benois de la Danse prize for choreography. The ballet opened the season again in 2008.[15] Storytelling aside, the use of the stage play was the most successful method through which the Bell Witch narrative reached new audiences.

For many students, fascination with the legend started early with the help of theatrical productions. In 1956, Nellie McCaslin published a book of twelve short plays intended for young people from eight to twelve years old. One of the plays concerned the Bell Witch and could be used by schools free of charge.[16] During the 1950s, the production of plays written both for and by young students was prevalent. The Children's Museum Dramatic Club of Jamaica Plain in Boston produced a folk play called *The Bell Witch of Tennessee*, featuring "a ghost and some lively square dances."[17] That decade, similar Bell Witch plays were performed by schools and children's theaters in California, Iowa, and Virginia, among other states.[18] During the 1960s and 1970s, similar productions for students were staged in New Jersey, Nebraska, Kentucky, Tennessee, and other states.[19]

Colleges participated in Bell Witch theatrical productions as well. In 1912, students taking Bible classes during the Halloween season at Buford College in Nashville, Tennessee, studied the supernatural in scriptures and the divine authority of the Christ over demonics and the "spirit of evil." Following theological discussion, they watched a play called *The Bell Witch*. One student concluded that the Bell Witch is "a real story of the supernatural demonstration in Tennessee."[20] Other colleges around the country staged their own performances based on the legend. Lipscomb University in Nashville featured a student-authored folk drama. The State University of New York, Purchase, held cabaret performances in "street style" entertainment as a means of presenting the Bell Witch story. The Performing Arts Program at Western Piedmont Community College in North Carolina staged *The Bell Witch of Tennessee*. Kennesaw State University in Georgia put on *The Bell Witch and Other Legends: Ghostly Storytelling from the American South*. The play ran for six performances.[21] These are only a few of the colleges that have presented plays about the story.

Another institution with connections to the legend is Austin Peay State University in Clarksville, Tennessee. The city has close ties to the Bell Witch legend as it is just a few miles from Adams. Further, M. V. Ingram was the editor of a Clarksville newspaper when he published the Bell Witch book in 1894. The people of Clarksville were thus intimate with the folklore. During the 1987–1988 academic year, renowned Broadway playwright Arthur Kopit, moved to the university, where he held the Roy Acuff Chair of Excellence in the Creative Arts. At Austin Peay, he helped students research and write a play about the famous local legend. The work was called *The Bell Witch Variations, Part I: The Letters of Joshua Gardner*. The workshop performances ran from May 25 to May 30, 1987, at the APSU's Trahern Theatre and included a midnight performance.[22]

Two other important Bell Witch plays were written and performed from the 1970s until the end of the century. In 1974, the Nashville Children's Theatre received a grant from the Tennessee Arts Commission to help fund the writing of an original play on the legend of the Bell Witch.[23] The product became known as *Our Family Trouble: The Legend of the Bell Witch*, written by Audrey Campbell, who had been an actor at the Children's Theatre. As a psychology teacher, Campbell viewed the play as a case study. She remarked, "I think the witch could have been a projection of all the fears and repressed feelings—it was the Victorian era, after all. And it's been said that ghosts and witches disapproved of the invention of the electric lightbulb."[24]

The play became well-known and was reviewed by newspapers across the country, including publications in West Virginia, Hawaii, Idaho,

Wisconsin, Arizona, Missouri, and Tennessee. Most of these articles were printed in conjunction with Halloween and were borrowed from the *Nashville Tennessean* article, "Kate was No Ordinary Witch" and its interview with Audrey Campbell.[25] The play was also produced by the Actor's Playhouse in Nashville from October 15 to November 7, 1987.[26]

Another Bell Witch play that received significant attention from audiences in Middle Tennessee was *The Bell Witch Story*, written and directed by Ric White. The play premiered in 1998 and was performed by the Sumner County Tennessee players. *The Bell Witch Story* was produced (sometimes intermittently) until 2009 at different venues in Middle Tennessee.[27]

As storytelling, ballets, and stage plays helped spread the intrigue of the legend, some people kept the story alive through negative press. Though many skeptics debunked it, in so doing they brought attention to the folklore. Harry Houdini, the famous magician and escape artist was one of the most prominent Bell Witch skeptics. On March 11, 1924, Houdini stood on the stage of the Ryman Auditorium in Nashville and lectured against spiritualists, mediums, and the Bell Witch story.[28]

Other positive examples include a variety of mediums. The Upper Crust Café in Capita, Wisconsin, sponsored a display of paintings by Theron Caldwell Res entitled "The Bell Witch Series," works in oil and watercolor based on "the legend of a spirit that controlled a small Tennessee community in the 19th century."[29] Between 1938 and 1941, ventriloquist Paul Stadelman and his dummy, Windy Higgins, performed in nearly two hundred small-town theatres and in large cities such as Chicago and Salt Lake City. Stadelman was from Hopkinsville, Kentucky, and knew the Bell Witch story, which became an important part of his act.[30]

Through extensive study, continued storytelling, and the arts, the Bell Witch became a popular entity in the twentieth century. But the twenty-first century saw "Old Kate's" transition into a pop culture queen.

eight

POP CULTURE QUEEN

There are at least 35 books, thousands of websites
and half a dozen plays about the Bell Witch.
Now, there's a ballet.

—*Nashville Tennessean,*
October 12, 2003

Pop culture keeps the legend of the Bell Witch alive

—*Sioux City Journal* (IA),
October 25, 2003

The Bell Witch—grandmother of today's
cinematic poltergeist and others as well.

—*Munster Times* (IN),
October 2, 2010

Oh yes, the Bell Witch is a true ghost story.
True in the sense that *something* happened, was
documented, passed into legend and history.
At least the *story* of the Bell Witch is true.

—JOHN F. D. TAFF,
The Bell Witch

The Bell Witch can be accurately described today as a "pop culture queen"; but what exactly is popular culture? Pop culture is generally recognized by members of a society as a set of practices, beliefs, and objects that are dominant or prevalent at a given point in time. Popular culture also encompasses the activities and feelings produced as a result of interaction with these dominant objects. In the category of entertainment, some of the most important media are radio, music, books, television, film, and more recently podcasts and websites. By the late twentieth century, American pop culture emerged as a dominant force shaping pop culture in much of the rest of the world.[1] Along the way, the Bell Witch has evolved into a worldwide pop culture entity.

RADIO

Before television was wildly available, the radio was a major source of entertainment and news for millions of Americans. The first licensed radio broadcast came from KDKA in Pittsburgh on November 2, 1920, and featured the Harding-Cox presidential election returns. By 1925, there were 2.5 million radios in America and 220 radio stations. NBC radio started in 1926, followed by CBS in 1928.[2]

It did not take long for the Bell Witch to arrive in homes across the United States via radio. WSM radio in Nashville was a fifty-thousand-watt station and could be heard in several states beyond Tennessee. On May 30, 1937, the station broadcasted a skit entitled, "Bell Witch: American's No. 1 Ghost Story," written by Marshal Morgan and featuring forty voice actors. Its promoters declared that, "It promises to be one of the highlights . . . and will bring to many ears the bewitching bits of fantasy, fiction or fact that have excited Tennesseans for more than a century." This was the first of several WSM broadcasts about the legend.[3]

Radio stations in other cities followed suit and began to air Bell Witch stories. One of the most prominent broadcasts was part of a series called "Hidden History" based on a collection of "distinctive American folktales" in the Library of Congress and adapted to radio by Bernard Victor Dryer.[4] This program was aired by radio stations in Richmond (VA), Louisville (KY), Madison (WI), Sioux City (IA), and other cities.[5] In 1946, station KWK in St. Louis presented "The Story of the Bell Witch" as part of the "Exploring the Unknown" series.[6]

MUSIC

Music is as old as humankind, and most people find the sound of the human voice blended with instruments highly compelling. Often the best way to tell a story is through song. Thus, it is not surprising that the already popular Bell Witch story would be recorded in verse. The first such song to be recorded and receive critical acclaim was country music star Merle Kilgore's "The Bell Witch" in 1964. One reviewer called the song a "catchy folk tune" and compared Kilgore to folk song legend Jimmie Rodgers.[7]

Twenty or so years later, the Bell Witch inspired a very different musical adaptation with the Danish heavy metal band Mercyful Fate. The band was formed in 1981, and in 1993 released a well-received album called In *the Shadows*," which included a song called "The Bell Witch." The opening lyrics proclaim, "Back in Tennessee, I saw a family haunted by an entity. It was a tragedy in another century."[8]

Closer to Bell Witch territory, in 1986, a band called The Shakers formed in Nashville with plans to write songs based on the famous Tennessee legend. They subsequently became one of Music City's most popular rock bands. In 1988, the group released *Living in the Shadow of a Spirit*, which featured three songs inspired by the legend: "Queen of the Haunted Dell," "The Healing Hymn," and "Hymn to Kate."[9]

Formed in 2010, Bell Witch, a doom metal band from Seattle released two albums—"Mirror Reaper" and "Four Phantoms"—to positive reviews. The group also received high praise from newspapers for its live performances in New York, California, Canada, and elsewhere. On a 2018 concert tour, the band also performed in Iceland, Belgium, and the Netherlands.[10] Further, a bar in Bellingham, Washington, named "The Shakedown" publicized a future Bell Witch band appearance at the establishment this way: "So Adult, Totalizer Devilry, Bell Witch and guests." The Bell Witch legend had reached the followers of doom metal music.[11] The supernatural was prevalent in short stories, novels and movies, naturally it would also appear in music.

BOOKS

The written word is even more important than the radio and music in understanding people's fascination concerning the Bell Witch legend.

To understand why, we must try to reconcile the allure that the feeling of fear holds for many people. We like being scared, provided we know that we are safe. In his classic essay on the genre, "Supernatural Horror in Literature," H. P. Lovecraft wrote: "The oldest and strongest emotion of mankind is fear, and the oldest and strongest kind of fear is fear of the unknown. These facts few psychologists will dispute, and their admitted truth must establish for all time the genuineness and dignity of the weirdly horrible tales as a literary form."[12] Lovecraft's observation certainly applies to the Bell Witch. Beginning with Ingram's book in 1894, several books have been printed about the legend. This suggests that for one hundred years, despite the "fear factor," there has been an audience eager to read about the witch.

Articles about the phenomena were published at a steady pace through the twentieth century, but few books about the story during this period were published until the 1990s. (One notable exception is Ruth Ellen Quillen's 1979 book, *The Bell Witch.*) This dry spell changed dramatically in the 1990s, and since then, over a dozen Bell Witch books have been published, at times to very positive reviews. While some of these works have been mentioned in earlier chapters, the following is a partial list of recent books on this subject:

1994: Barbara Michaels, *Other Worlds*

1994: Charles Edmund Price, *The Infamous Bell Witch of Tennessee*

1997: Brent Monahan, *The Bell Witch*

1999: Troy Taylor, *Season of the Witch*

2000: Pat Fitzhugh, *The Bell Witch: The Full Account*

2003: Timothy Henson, *The Black Patch Bells: The Story of John and Lucy Bell*

2005: Robert Maughon, *Bell Witch: The Movie Novel*

2007: Dewey Edwards, *Something Wicked: The Bell Witch Phenomenon*

2008: Camille Moffitt Headley, *Bell Witch: The Truth Explored*

2013: John Taff, *The Bell Witch*

2014: Jeff Hocxenheimer and John Howell, *The Secrets of the Bell Witch*

2015: Sean Castell, et al., *The Bell Witch Project*

2015: Dr. Jim Brooks, *Bell Witch Stories You Never Heard*

2015: William Gay, *Little Sister Death*

2016: Kyle T. Cobb Jr., *The Truth of the Bell Witch*

Some of these books were reviewed in newspapers in both the United States and Canada. Brent Monahan's book, for instance, was reviewed in Canada in the *Nangima Daily News* (BC).[13] Over the decades, dozens of reviews of Bell Witch books helped spread the legend nationally and internationally. Some writers also published Bell Witch books and articles for younger readers. By doing so, they introduced the story to a new generation.[14]

The Bell Witch also made appearances in fiction books not explicitly about the legend. Heather Graham is a prolific mystery writer whose books have been read by millions of readers. In her novel *Haunted*, two people carry on this discussion: "Haven't you ever heard of the Bell Witch of Tennessee? They say that even old Andrew Jackson was afraid of her, that she pulled people's hair and threw the children around and even caused the death of the master of the house."[15] The legend continued to extend its spell on readers.

FILM

This fascination, or "hex" if you will, also drew people who like to watch horror movies and videos. Monsters, witches, zombies, vampires, and countless other creatures have been popular with viewers since the dawn of cinema.[16] According to Charles Derry, "Horror films connect with our profound and subconscious need to deal with things that frighten us." He adds that, while watching a film, "screaming can actually provide a healthy catharsis."[17]

Proof of an obsession with the feeling of fear is evident in the box office performances of horror movies on the big screen. In 2018 alone, horror films in the United States grossed over $900,000,000 and entertained nearly 100,000,000 viewers. In 2019, the numbers were almost $750,000,000 with over 80,000,000 viewers.[18]

Zombie films are among the most watched subgenre of horror movies. The first zombie movies screened in the 1920s and 1930s. Even so, these films did not become the dominant form of horror movies until the twenty-first century. Since then, over a dozen zombie movie have made it to the big screen.[19] There is a clear link between the rise of zombie culture and the origins of the Bell Witch legend. In both cases, each has been celebrated in books, television, music, and film. Each also developed in eras of social and cultural unease. In short, there is considerable overlap in those who enjoy the zombie genre and eager followers of the Bell Witch legend.

In *Dark Dreams,* Charles Derry asserts that "Horror films speak, therefore, to the shared fears, to a culture's anxieties."[20] The Bell Witch legend developed two hundred years ago when people in middle Tennessee were experiencing a massive religious revival, some even wondered if Satan was playing a role in the movement. The legend developed in an era when an earthquake, comet, or volcano compelled people to wonder if the apocalypse was truly nigh. The zombie craze also arose in a difficult time in American history. Citizens experienced the collective horror of the terrorist attack on American soil on September 11, 2001, prolonged wars in Iraq and Afghanistan, and the worst recession since the 1930s. When people feel anxious, stories about supernatural entities serve as an appealing means of escapism.

In the first two decades of this century, several Bell Witch movies and films claiming to be "documentaries" were produced. Some of them were:

2003: *The Official Bell Witch Video*
2004: *Bell Witch Haunting*
2005: *Bell Witch, The Movie*
2005: *An American Haunting*
2008: *The Bell Witch Legend*
2013: *The Bell Witch Haunting*

These films represent only a few of the hundreds of films about the Bell Witch, which helped keep the mythology alive. One film that made it to the "big screen," however, is deserving of special attention. *An American Haunting* (2005) was inspired by Brent Monahan's novel *The Bell Witch: An American Haunting* and featured well-known film actors. Sissy Spacek portrayed Lucy Bell, Donald Sutherland acted the part of John Bell, and Rachel Hurd-Wood played Betsy Bell. The movie opened the 37th annual Nashville Film Festival in April 2006; afterward, the film was reviewed by newspapers across the United States, Canada, and even Guam. *An American Haunting* was released to DVD in 2013.[21]

Each of these films, large screen and small, shared the story with countless viewers. The same can be said for television. In 1948, less than 3 percent of American households owned a television. Only four years later,

45 percent owned television sets. Today, the average household has more than one television. The prevalence of this invention brought the stories into millions of households around the planet.[22] It introduced millions of viewers to the Bell Witch and reminded millions of others of the story they already knew.

One of the first Bell Witch TV shows aired in 1955— a folklore piece titled "The Bell Witch of Tennessee and Mississippi" on WTOK-TV in Meridian, Mississippi. Twenty years later, WSM-TV broadcast a documentary called *The Bell Witch*. The new century began with renewed interest in the legend.[23] In 2000, the Learning Channel's series "Night Visitors" ran a program called "The Vengeful Bell Witch of Tennessee," and in 2002 another episode called "The Bell Witch: A 19th-Century Teenage Vampire." Each program ran several times.[24] In 2005 and 2006, PBS aired a series called "Southern Haunts." One of the segments was about the Bell Witch.[25] From 2010 until 2019, Kentucky Educational Television (KET) ran Zac Adams's video *The Bell Witch Legend* over sixty times.[26] Broadcast in 2015, the Travel Channel's "Cursed: The Bell Witch" was perhaps one of the most watched programs related to the legend. It consisted of seven episodes and was reviewed by dozens of newspapers in the United States and Canada.[27] In 2018, the Travel Channel broadcast "Haunted Live: Bell Witch," and the following year aired "Ghost Adventures: Bell Witch Cave."[28]

INTERNET

The roots of the internet, or "World Wide Web," can be traced to the 1960s. The first web page in the United States was introduced at Stanford University in 1991.[29] Within a few years, articles about the legend began to circulate on the internet. Newspapers, which were now accessible online, also carried articles about this new way to seek information. From this beginning, the internet became a dominant force in the information and entertainment fields. Where the Bell Witch folklore is concerned, hundreds of websites, webcasts, podcasts, and videos feature information. The day before Halloween in 1999, the *Asbury Park Press* (NJ) reprinted an article from the *Louisville Courier-Journal* concerning information about the Bell Witch on the internet. The reporter wrote, "BE AFRAID: Be very afraid if you go poking around in the dark corners of the world wide web, you will find many scary things."[30]

The Bell Witch name has also attached to items with no connection to folklore or the legend. The Miskatonic Brewing Company in Darien, Illinois, produced a beer called "Bell Witch."[31] A horse by the same name raced at Aqueduct, Pimlico, and other racetracks.[32] In Springfield, Tennessee, a company named Nature Tails, a pet and lifestyle brand, featured dog treats called "Bell Witch Bites."[33] As the fame of the Bell Witch grew, an increasing number of people in Adams realized that the legend could be economically beneficial to the city. This fact will be explored in the next chapter.

nine

WANT TO EXPERIENCE THE BELL WITCH?
COME TO ADAMS

A couple years ago, Hollywood made an awful movie
called "An American Haunting" about the incident
[The Bell Witch story]. This play puts the movie to
shame. [Referring to the "SPIRIT" play in Adams, TN]

—JOEL PIERSON,
Martinsville (IN) *Reporter-Times*,
November 16, 2008

During the early twenties of the past century,
a mystery known as The Bell Witch appeared
in Robertson County, Tenn., near what is at present
the little town of Adams.

—HARRIET PARKS MILLER,
The Bell Witch of Middle Tennessee

In the course of its existence, Adams has had
its claim to fame, but nothing would ever compare
to or outlive the infamous legacy left by that
mysterious entity known as the Bell Witch.

—DEWEY EDWARDS,
Something Wicked: The Bell Witch Phenomenon

Ultimately, after gossip, storytelling, newspaper and magazine articles,
books, music, dance, plays, television, radio, movies, and the internet,

the search to understand the Bell Witch story begins and ends in Red River/Adams, Tennessee. Outside media influences notwithstanding, the town has truly made the legend its own, and has in the process become irrevocably linked to the tale's longevity. Several books and newspaper articles have spotlighted Adams's enduring reputation as a supernatural "hotspot." A *Clarksville Leaf-Chronicle* article entitled "Making Adams Famous" called attention to recent Bell Witch books, plays, and movies.[1] Further, a *National Geographic* publication listed the Bell Witch cave as one of the world's most supernatural places.[2] Adams's identity as the home of the Bell Witch has become a force of its own.

Folklorist Elke Dettmer called attention to the economic power of folklore. When people become tourists, they can have a positive effect on the economies of the areas they visit.[3] In 2010, Margo Fosnes, executive director of the Robertson County Chamber of Commerce, used statistics from the University of Tennessee Tourism Institute to estimate that "each tourism dollar translates into $2.10 of additional spending in the local economy," and that "Robertson County collects nearly $1,000,000 annually in local sales tax on tourism-related expenditures."[4] Fosnes added that "the city of Adams knows well the importance of tourism dollars and the town and local merchants take great advantage of the notoriety of the Bell Witch." A decade earlier, a newspaper article supported this idea in observing, "Whether they believe it or not, the 600 people of Adams depend in part on the Bell Witch—named Kate—for their economic health."[5]

The prosperity that the legend brought to Adams relied upon the eagerness of many local residents to tell and hear Bell Witch stories— what a 1937 newspaper called their desire to tell "weird witch tales."[6] In researching his 2005 film, "An American Haunting," Courtney Solomon was surprised to find how many local people still believed that "something is still awry around the old Bell homestead." He added, "At least 15 people told me stories about things that happened to them or to a close family member or to a close friend. It's amazing that it has lasted this long." In support of this observation, John Mantooth, a local schoolteacher and principal asserted, "Most everybody around here has at least one Bell Witch story."[7]

Even so, not all local citizens, past and present, have been happy with the town's supernatural reputation. In 1939, A. L. Dorsey, a Robertson County attorney and historian, wrote a letter to an acquaintance downplaying the importance of the legend. He quoted a local citizen who doubted that "any of the Bell family believed in 'Old Kate.'" Dorsey also ventured his belief that "Such publicity for Robertson County is not very good, but the people here do not appear to care anything about it one way or the other."[8]

Dorsey was a good historian, but wrong about the resilience and economic importance of the Bell Witch legend to the town of Adams and Robertson County. Numerous organizations and businesses adopted the Bell Witch name, while the Bell Witch Quilt Festival, Bell Witch Riding Club and Horse Show, Bell Witch Basketball Classic, Bell Witch Open presented by Dynamic Discs represent only a small sample of events in Adams that have capitalized on the town's supernatural fame.[9] Though many organizations that used the Bell Witch name did not last long, some endured for years or decades.

THE BELL WITCH CAVE

Visitors were coming to the Bell Witch Cave decades before it became a commercial endeavor for its owners. As discussed earlier, a physical landmark is one of the foundations for an enduring ghost story. In this case, the cave itself also serves as an attraction for those seeking a "spooky" experience. Pilgrimages to the cave as early as the 1930s are a testament to the allure of the supernatural, even before the arrival of modern tourism advertisement. In August 1935, a local Sunday school class picnicked at the cave, as did Boy Scout Troop 70 from Hermitage, Tennessee, the next month. In 1937, the freshman class at Bell High School in Adams enjoyed a trip to the cave, and the next year, the school's science class hiked to the cave and searched for rocks. In 1937 a group of visitors reported seeing an apparition at the cave that some believed to be the Bell Witch. In the summer of 1939, residents from Adairville, Kentucky, enjoyed spending time at the Bell Witch Camp near Adams.[10]

In the 1950s, many writers focused on the Bell Witch cave as a tourist destination, while tourism sections in newspapers country-wide featured articles on the destination. As the country moved into the twenty-first century, television shows and the internet also focused on the cave as a supernatural tourist spot. Since the cave was located on the Red River, local entrepreneurs opened a campground and started businesses to rent canoes, kayaks, and floats on the river.[11]

In 2008, the National Park Service added the Bell Witch cave to the National Register of Historic Places, declaring that "The Bell Witch cave is unique among Tennessee's tourist caves. Significant in entertainment/recreation, the cave has been the focus of not only tours, but on ongoing folklore. The legend of the Bell Witch is known beyond the boundaries of the state, and historically, visitors have come from far away to visit the site,"[12] This recognition was reported in newspapers across the country.[13]

The State of Tennessee also recognized the importance of the Bell Witch cave in its 1961 publication on the state's most important caves.[14] The State Department of Tourism touted Adams and the cave as a primary tourist attraction.[15] Although it did not specifically mention the cave, the Tennessee Historical Commission erected a historical marker in Adams celebrating the Bell Witch legend. Marker 3C38 reads: "To the north was the farm of John Bell, an early prominent settler from North Carolina. According to legend, his family was harried during the early 19th century by the famous Bell Witch. She kept the household in turmoil, assaulted Bell, and drove off Betsy Bell's suitor. Even Andrew Jackson, who came to investigate, retreated to Nashville after his coach wheels stopped mysteriously. Many visitors to the house saw the furniture crash about them and heard her shriek, sing, and curse." According to one article, it was the "only marker in the US . . . erected to a witch."[16]

The property, especially the cave, attracted a growing number of visitors through the decades of the twentieth century. In 1964, William "Bims" Eden purchased 105 acres of the old Bell farm, including the cave. He soon realized that conducting cave tours could be a lucrative proposition. He said that he "couldn't farm anymore because most of his time was taken up being a tour guide." He was a gifted storyteller and included personal encounters with the supernatural as part of his tours. Inevitably, he started charging a fee to tour the cave and parts of the old Bell farm.[17] In 1993, Chris and Walter Kirby purchased the cave and surrounding land and continued the cave tours. They also started a canoe and kayak rental business.[18]

THE THRESHERMEN'S SHOW

The cave was not the only factor in making Adams a tourist destination. Over the last fifty years, several Adams-based organizations have brought tens of thousands of people to the town. The Tennessee-Kentucky

Threshermen's Show had its debut in Adams on August 20–22, 1970. The association was founded "for the purpose of recapturing through act and display, the spirit of the days when 'steam was king.'" The show featured steam engines, threshers, a sawmill, old tractors, antique cars, church services, music, and campgrounds.[19] It has been presented in Adams every year since 1970. The first show drew five thousand people from twenty-six states. In the years since, thousands of people from dozens of states have gathered annually for the festival. From the first year, and for most years since, Bell Witch storytelling has been one of the show's most popular events. William Turner, discussed earlier in this study, spoke at the first show and many of them since.[20]

BELL WITCH BLUEGRASS FESTIVAL

The first annual festival was held in August 1979. This two-day event featured several local talents and well-known bluegrass performers including Wilma Lee Cooper, Jimmy Martin, and the Stonemans as well as competitions with cash prizes for fiddling, clogging, harmonica, banjo, mandolin, guitar, and dobro.[21] Up until 2014, the festival included the Bell Witch Old Time Fiddlers Contest, a celebration of bluegrass music. Using the term "Bell Witch" as a part of the events helped attract tourists to an area noted for the legend.[22]

BELL WITCH OPRY AND ANTIQUE MALL

Kenneth and Nina Seeley had great expectations for Adams, the Bell Witch legend, and local tourism.[23] In the late 1970s, they purchased the old Bell schoolhouse in Adams and turned it into the Bell Witch Village and Antique Mall. The mall became a favorite stop for antique hunters and was included in guidebooks for "treasure seekers."[24] In 1981, the Seelys started the Bell Witch Opry in the same building as the antique mall. They envisioned the Opry becoming a "showplace for old-time country music," as both Seelys had close ties to the genre. Ken was recognized by the Smithsonian Institution as a distinguished country music entertainer, and Nina was a former Nashville musician who had played with Carl Perkins and Eddy Arnold.[25]

The Opry, which attracted performers and music fans from out of state, played on Saturday nights in Adams and was broadcasted live by

WDBL radio station in Springfield. In one instance, a band from Minnesota played at the Opry, drawing guests from as far away as Adelaide, Australia.[26] A highlight for Adams and the Opry occurred in 1984 when a television crew from the Norwegian Broadcasting Corporation arrived in Adams to film the Opry as part of a documentary about tourist attractions in Tennessee. Director Erik Dieseo claimed that he had read several Bell Witch books in preparation for the filming. While in the state, the crew also visited the Grand Ole Opry, Jim Reeves Museum, and the Country Music Hall of Fame in Nashville. They also did tapings in Memphis and New Orleans.[27]

Unfortunately, the Seely's next step in their vision for Adams was beyond their reach. With some other locals, the Seelys planned the Bell Witch Mystery City and Red River Movie Complex. At the cost of $110,000,000, the complex was to open in 1988 with a 4,000–6,000 seat Bell Witch Opry House, a movie-making complex with a sound stage, recording and video studios, a hundred-room hotel, restaurants, campsites, and an adventure cave. One promoter claimed that it would be "the biggest entertainment complex for training on the east coast." As it turned out, the plan was never more than a dream.[28] Sadly, Kenneth and Nina Seelys' lives ended in tragedy: he died in 1986 from a self-inflicted gunshot wound at the age of sixty, and Nina died in 2003 in a housefire. Though their vision was never fully realized, their ambition for the region spurred renewed enthusiasm for the lore. Their deaths were reported in newspapers in Tennessee and beyond.[29]

PARANORMAL SEEKERS

Since the turn of the last century, a growing number of individuals, groups, and organizations have journeyed to Adams in search of the Bell Witch and the Bell Witch story. For decades, the Bell Witch cave was the focus of many visitors, but recently a growing number of people have shown interest in both the story and the possibility of a personal supernatural experience. Adams has also seen numerous groups interested in filming movies, television shows, or documentaries, though the number of inquiries is too great to adequately document.

Pat Fitzhugh and other members of the Bell Witch Historical Society held the first "Katefest" in Adams in 1998. The 2002 Katefest featured, among other things, a keynote address, a banquet, and an "expert panel discussion" about the Bell Witch. The gathering only lasted for a few years.[30] The Gateway Paranormal Society, formed in 2008, claims to be "one of the most distinguished paranormal research groups in the world." They investigate hauntings, UFOs, and other mysteries, and on April 13, 2019, held a meeting in Adams to discuss the Bell Witch phenomenon.[31]

SPIRIT

Sometimes an opportunity presents itself due to good timing. This was the case with David Alford, the Bell Witch story, and Adams in the early 2000s. Alford grew up in Adams and went to Jo Byrns High School, where he developed a passion for music and the performing arts. From there, he attended Martin College, Austin Peay State University, and then the Julliard School for Drama in New York City. He grew up hearing Bell Witch stories and, in 1987, while at Austin Peay, portrayed Joshua Gardner in Arthur Kopit's play *The Bell Witch Variations*. After leaving Julliard, he acted in plays, television shows, and movies. In the early 2000s, he was a founder and artistic director of Mockingbird Theatre.[32]

Following his interest in the Bell Witch legend, Alford wrote the play SPIRIT: *The Authentic Bell Witch of Tennessee*. A local group called the SPIRIT Support Committee was formed to raise funds and help bring the play to the stage. Explaining his vision for the play, Alford said, "We don't solve the mystery. Instead there are dramatizations of key moments in the story." He explained, "It's designed to be a sort of community event," and hoped it would "grow into a long-running outdoor drama." And it did. Alford gave the play to the city of Adams.[33] SPIRIT premiered at the outdoor Bell School Pavilion in Adams on October 16, 2002, and ran on October 17, 18, 30, and 31. SPIRIT also showed at the Nashville Children's Theatre for seven performances in November of that year.[34]

A unique feature of SPIRIT is that Bell family members were often actors in the play. Carney Bell was a lineal descendant of John Bell and portrayed his ancestor. Over the years, three generations of Bell descendants have acted in SPIRIT. From its inception, the play received immediate acclaim. The "Tennies" award recognizes the best of Nashville theatre each year. In 2002, David Alford and Rene Copeland received the awards for best directors, and Jeff D. Boyet and Carol Ponder were recognized as best supporting actors. An Associated Press article praised the play and noted that it was the only Bell Witch play authorized by the Bell family.[35]

The next two decades brought much success and a few changes for *SPIRIT*, which was produced every fall from 2002 to 2019, with the exception of 2005. That year, Alford wanted to make some changes to the play, and so Ric White's play *The Bell Witch Story* was presented instead.[36] Also, due to the Covid epidemic, no performances were held in 2020 and 2021. In 2004 the governing body of the play changed when Community Spirit, Inc. (CSI) was formed to replace Mockingbird Theatre. All members of CSI volunteer their time and talents to make the play as good as possible.

Two other changes came with the expansion of the Bell Witch Fall Festival. Alford wrote a second play called *Smoke: A Ballad of the Night Riders*, which revolves around the actions of the "Tobacco Night Riders" in the first decade of the 1900s when tobacco farmers used violence to rebel against the American Tobacco Company and other tobacco companies. These events took place in the same area that produced the Bell Witch folklore. *Smoke* debuted in 2010. In 2015, CSI launched "Red River Tales: History, Folklore, Stories, Music," a free event that which features Bell Witch stories. Since 2002, over twenty-five thousand people have attended *SPIRIT* in Adams and thousands have viewed *Smoke* and "Red River Tales." After seeing *SPIRIT*, Joel Pierson, theatre writer for the *Martinsville Reporter-Times* (IN), wrote, "I would like to see something similar in Bloomington (IN). Not 'SPIRIT' necessarily, since the Adams group does that show justice. Whatever it is, it should be a subject that inspires a lot of local pride, something with some history, and a good story to tell then tell it every year. If people have already seen it, make them want to come back. If done well, it can be the start of an annual tradition that brings people from miles away; just as 'SPIRIT' brought me to Adams, Tennessee on a chilly Halloween night."[37]

Pierson was right. People have come to Adams from other states and countries to see *SPIRIT*. Many attendees are return audience members, and some have come every year since 2002. Adams and the Bell Witch legend have a symbiotic relationship. Without Red River/Adams the Bell Witch legend would not have survived for over two hundred years; and without the Bell Witch, few people in the country—and the world—would have heard of Adams.

Epilogue

I do not claim that I can tell a good story as it ought to be told. I only claim to know a story ought to be told.

—MARK TWAIN,
"How to Tell a Story," 1897

As long as they speak your name, you will never die.

—DANTE ALIGHIERI,
Inferno

It's not a lie if you believe it.

—GEORGE COSTANZA,
Seinfeld

Monsters are real and ghosts are real, too.
They live inside us.

—STEPHEN KING,
Facebook, November 26, 2013

Of all the eerie tales ever told, none is more terrifying than the sinister story of the Bell Witch. And every word of it is true.

—ALLEN SPRAGGETT,
"The Unexplained," *Province Vancouver* (BC),
September 14, 1973

In a recent article in the *Tennessee Magazine,* Bill Carey asked, "What is it about Robertson County and ghosts?"[1] The answer is simple: the Bell Witch. The legend has spanned two centuries and circulated across much of the world. The story began with gossip and storytelling and ultimately made its way to the internet.

It is ironic to me that I wrote the majority of this book in the bicentennial year of John Bell's death and the year of COVID-19. The Bell Witch and the virus both brought fear into the lives of millions of people. But the pandemic also afforded me the time to write. My goal in writing this book was to answer three questions: What do people believe that they cannot prove? Why do they believe what they cannot prove? And, how did the Bell Witch story become known worldwide? To these, I add the following: Is the story true? Does it make a significant difference if it is true or not? I spent part of Chapter 1 exploring the "what and why" of belief. For our purposes here, it can be concluded that we believe what we need to believe to help us understand and fit into the world around us. The "why" is easier. Simply put, we are human. As sapiens, we go through life compelled to ask why. Sometimes, however, the need to answer these questions is overridden by the desire to take things at face value, no matter how irrational. In short, the story became worldwide because it is a good and entertaining tale.

The questions about truth are harder to answer. The Bell Witch folklore is a good example that truth and belief are not the same thing. We believe what we need or want to be true, but truth does not surrender to belief. Even so, the Bell Witch story has survived for over two centuries. I reckon it will survive this book and many more to come. After all, for many people, storytelling, myths, and legends are more powerful than truth.

I leave the final words to two Bell Witch writers. John F. D. Taff concluded, "The story of the Bell Witch is a good ghost story . . . a great tome. Oh yes, the Bell Witch is a *true* ghost story. True in the sense that *something* happened, was documented, passed into legend and history. At least, the *story* of the Bell Witch is true."[2]

A. S. Mott probably gave the best answer to queries about the truth, proclaiming: "After almost two centuries have passed it is clear that this mystery shall never be answered. We will never know for sure who the 'Bell Witch' really was, why it did what it did or even if it really existed at all, but the truth is that with a story as fascinating as this, it really doesn't matter if a few questions are left to forever linger in our heads."[3]

Notes

Chapter 1

1. Other areas have claimed the Bell Witch Story as their own, as will be discussed later in the narrative.

2. Phillip Pullman, *Daemon Voices: On Stories and Storytelling* (Oxford, UK: David Ficking Books, 2017), 54.

3. "The Neuroscience: Why Your Brain Loves Good Storytelling," https://www.humanizethebrand.com/neuroscience-storytelling/.

4. Reynolds Price, *A Palpable God* (New York: Athenaeum, 1978), 3.

5. Ferris Jabr, "The Story of Storytelling," *Harper's Magazine*, March 1, 2019, 39.

6. Jmu.edu/counselingstr/files.

7. Upliftconnect.com/the-power-of-sharing-stories/.

8. Jane Polley, ed., *American Folklore and Legend: The Saga of our Heroes and Heroines, Our Braggers, Boosters and Mad Men, Our Beliefs and Superstitions* (Pleasantville, NY: *Reader's Digest*, 1978), 6.

9. Ibid., 134–35.

10. Michael Owen Jones, ed., *Putting Folklore to Use* (Lexington: University Press of Kentucky, 1994), 13.

11. Arthur Palmer Hudson and Pete Kyle McCarter, "The Bell Witch of Tennessee and Mississippi," *The Journal of American Folklore, 47, no.183* (Jan–Mar 1934): 45–63.

12. For more information, see Betty Sue Flowers, *Joseph Campbell: The Power of Myth with Bill Moyers* (New York: Doubleday, 1988.)

13. Harari, *Sapiens*, 27.

14. Ibid., 163.

15. Nicholas Cards and Patrick Gerster, *Myth and the American Experience*, 2 vols. (Beverly Hills: Glencoe Press, 1973), 2.

16. For more information, see Marion Gibson, *Witchcraft Myths in American Culture* (Abingdon, UK: Routledge, 2007).

17. Harari, *Sapiens*, 22–24. See also, Sophia Gottfried, "The Science Behind Why People Gossip," http://time.com/5680457/why-do-people-gossip/.

18. B. A. Botkin, ed. *A Treasury of Southern Folklore, Ballads, Traditions, and Folkways of the People of the South* (New York: Crown Publishers, 1949), 417.

19. Glen Hinson and William Ferris, eds., *The New Encyclopedia of Southern Folklore*, vol. 14, Folklife (Chapel Hill: University of North Carolina Press, 2006).

20. *Murfreesboro Daily News-Journal*, March 4, 1984, 34.

21. Floyd E. Randall, *More Great Southern Mysteries* (Little Rock, AR: August House Publishers, Inc., 1990), 26–29.

22. Rick Bragg, "Free Spirits," *Southern Living*, October 2019, 124.

23. Emma B. Miles, *The Spirit of the Mountains* (New York: James Pott, 1905), 108–17.

24. Botkin, *Treasury of Southern Folklore*, 470. For a broader view, see Wayland Hand's *Popular Beliefs and Superstitions from North Carolina* (Durham, NC: Duke University Press, 1977). See also, Sue Hardin, *Devil's Tramping Ground and Other North Carolina Mystery Stories* (Chapel Hill: University of North Carolina Press, 1949). For a wider view, see Tom Peete Cross's article, "Witchcraft in North Carolina," Studies in Philology XVI, no. 3 (July 1919): 236–87. Cross explores many similarities between the Bell Witch legend and other legends in the United States and England.

25. William Lynwood Montell, *The Tales of Kentucky Ghosts* (Lexington: University Press of Kentucky, 2010). See also, J. T. Gooch, *The Pennyrile History, Stories, Legends* (Roswell, GA: Whippoorwill Publications, 1982).

26. Compiled and written by The Federal Writers' Project of the Work Projects Administration (WPA) for the State of Tennessee, *Tennessee: A Guide to the State* (New York: Viking Press, 1939), 19. See also, James G. Leyborn, *The Scotch-Irish: A Social History* (Chapel Hill: University of North Carolina Press, 1976) and David Hackett Fischer, *Albion's Seed: Four British Folkways in America* (Oxford: Oxford University Press, 1989).

27. "Don't Roam Afield Writer Advised," *Chattanooga Times*, January 20, 1940.

28. Ursula Smith Beach, *Along the Warioto: A History of Montgomery County, Tennessee* (Nashville, TN: McQuiddy, 1965), 333.

29. Heidi Hein, "Bell Witch Legend Lives on in Folklore of Tennessee," *Clarksville Leaf-Chronicle*, January 24, 1989.

30. Florence Wilson, "Ghosts Walk in Many Tennessee Homes," *Nashville Banner Magazine*, September 5, 1937. For books about supernatural events in

Tennessee that include the Bell Witch legend, see James R. Aswell, *God Bless the Devil: Tennessee Folktales* (New York: Van Rees Press, 1940); Christopher K. Coleman, *Strange Tales of the Dark and Bloody Ground: Authentic Accounts of Restless Spirits, Haunted Honkytonks and Eerie Events in Tennessee* (Nashville, TN: Rutledge Hill Press, 1998); Bob Galbreath, *Tennessee Redberry Tales* (Whites Creek, TN: Whites Creek Press, 1986); A. S. Mott, *Ghost Stories of Tennessee* (Auburn, WA: Lone Pine Publishing, 2005); Charles Edwin Price, *Haunted Tennessee* (Johnson City, TN: Overmountain Press, 1995).

31. For more information about the early formation of language, see Tamim Ansgry, *The Invention of Yesterday: A 50,000-Year History of Human Culture, Conflict and Connection* (New York: Public Affairs, 2019).

32. Yolanda G. Reid and Rick S. Gregory, *Home of the World's Finest: Robertson County, Tennessee* (Paducah, KY: Turner Publishing Company, 1996), 125.

33. Richard Russo, "The Lives of Others, When Imagination Becomes Appropriation," *Harper's Magazine*, June 2020, 31.

34. Iona Opie and Moira Tatem, eds., *A Dictionary of Superstitions* (New York: Barnes and Noble, 1989). See also, John Brockman, ed., *What We Believe But Cannot Prove: Today's Leading Thinkers on Science in the Age of Certainty* (New York: Harper Perennial, 2006). Brockman's book shows that even scientists sometimes believe what they cannot prove.

35. Paranormal America, 2017 Chapman University Survey of American Fears, 2017, http://blogs.chapman.edu/wilkinson/2017/10/11/paranormal-america-2017/.

36. Brian Regal and Frank J. Esposito, *The Secret History of the Jersey Devil: How Quakers, Hucksters, and Benjamin Franklin Created a Monster* (Baltimore, MD: Johns Hopkins University Press, 2018).

37. Alexis Coe, You Never Forget Your First: A Biography of George Washington (New York: Viking, 2020), xvii.

38. Jared Cohen, *Accidental Presidents: Eight Men Who Changed America* (New York: Simon and Schuster, 2019), 2. See also, John Sugden, *Tecumseh: A Life* (New York: Henry Holt, 1997), 256.

39. Timothy J. Redmond, "The Presidential Curse and the Election of 2020," *Skeptical Inquirer*, 43, no. 6 (2020): 40–41. See also, Joel Martin and William J. Birnes, *The Haunting of the Presidents: A Paranormal History of the U.S. Presidency* (Saybook, CT: Konecky & Konecky, 2003).

40. Matthew Goodman, *The Sun and the Moon and the Remarkable True Account of Hoaxers, Showmen, Dueling Journalists, and Lunar Man-Bats* (New York: Basic Books, 2008). See also, Tammy Painter, "The Great Moon Hoax," podcast audio, June 24, 2020, http://www.thebookowlpodcast.

41. Joshua Buhs, *Bigfoot: The Life and Times of a Legend* (Chicago: University of Chicago Press, 2009). See also, Daniel Taylor, *Something Hidden Behind the Ranges: A Himalayan Quest* (San Francisco: Mercury House, 1995); and David Childress, "Big Foot Nation: The History of Sasquatch in North America (Kemptom, IL: Adventures Unlimited Press, 2018).

42. Ben Crair, "Call of the Wildman: Why do Some People Still Want to Believe in Bigfoot?," *Smithsonian*, September 2018, 11–13. See also, "The Enduring Legend of Bigfoot," *The Week*, April 12, 2019, 10; Max Brooks, *Devolution: A First Hand Account Novel: Bigfoot Legend of the Ranier Massacre* (New York: Del Rey, 2020); and *The Week*, February 5, 2021, 6.

43. An example of the endurance of this tale through storytelling can be found in a book by a local Robertson County author Dewey Edwards, *Ghostly Whispers: A Collection of Ghostly Tales and Personal Encounters* (Self-published, 2019). Edwards included an article concerning Bigfoot sightings in Robertson County.

44. Michael McClendon, *Critter: Some Things Have Been Dug Up . . .* Down South (London, GB: Austin Macauley Publishers, 2020).

45. For more information about this tale, see John A. Keel, *The Mothman Prophecies* (New York: Saturday Review Press, 1975).

46. Henry H. Bauer, *The Enigma of Loch Ness: Making Sense of a Mystery* (Chicago: University of Illinois Press, 1986); Donald Prothero and Daniel Loxton, *Abominable Science: Origins of the Yeti, Nessie, and Other Famous Cryptids* (New York: Columbia University Press, 2013); "Nessie's Starring Role," *The Week*, October 25, 2013, 40–41.

47. Benson Bobrick, *The Fated Sky: Astrology in History* (New York: Simon and Schuster, 2005).

48. Christine Smallwood, "STARSTRUCK: In Uncertain Times, Astrology Makes a Comeback," *New Yorker*, October 28, 2019, 20–24.

49. *The Week*, June 14, 2019, 14; and "UFOs: The Pentagon's Secret Study," *The Week*, August 14, 2020, 19; and Gideon Lewis-Kraus, "The U.F.O. Papers: Why Did We Start Taking Unidentified Aerial Phenomena Seriously?," *The New Yorker*, May 10, 2021, 32–47.

50. (http://ufodigest.com)(article/bell-witch-0408) and Sean Casteel et al., *The Bell Witch Project: Poltergeists, Ghosts, Exorcism, and the Supernatural in Early American History* (New Brunswick, NJ: Global Communication, 2015).

51. J. T. Gooch, "The Little Green Men of Kelly," *The Pennyrile*, 84–92; and "Little Green Men of Kelly, Kentucky," *Madisonville Kentucky Messenger*, October 11, 2017. See also, Isabel Davis and Ted Bloecher, *Close Encounter at Kelly and Others of 1955* (Evanston, IL: Center for UFO Studies, 1978).

52. Owen Davies, ed., *The Haunted: A Social History of Ghosts*, 5 vols. (London, UK: Palgrave Macmillan, 2007); David C. Knight, *Poltergeists: Haunting and the Haunted (Philadelphia: Lippincott, 1972).* To explore the link between the Bell Witch and other ghost stories, see Colin Damon and Rowan Wilson, *World Famous True Ghost Stores* (Bristol, UK: Parragon Book Service, 1996), 23–25; and Daniel Cohen, *The Encyclopedia of Ghosts* (New York: Dodd, Mead, 1984), 157–63.

53. Ruiz F. Teofilo, *The Terror of History: On the Uncertainties of Life in Western Civilization* (Princeton, NJ: Princeton University Press, 2011); Ankar Bengt and Stuart Clark, *Witchcraft and Magic in Europe: Biblical and Pagan Societies* (Philadelphia: University of Philadelphia Press, 2001).

54. Marion Gipson, *Witchcraft Myths in American Culture* (Abingeon-on-Thames, UK: Routledge, 2007); and David Hackett Fischer, *Albion's Seed: Four British Folkways in America* (New York: Oxford University Press, 1989), 127, 189, 194, 341, 709–15.

55. John Demos, *Entertaining Satan: Witchcraft and the Culture of Early New England* (Oxford: Oxford University Press, 1982); and Stacey Schiff, *The Witches: Salem in 1692* (New York: Little, Brown, 2015).

56. Juliet Diaz, *Embrace the Witch Within* (Carlsbad, CA: Hay House, 2019); and Bianca Bosker, "The Witching Hour," *Atlantic*, March 2020, 14–16.

57. For an academic take on belief, see Dean Burnett, *The Idiot Brain: A Neuroscientist Explains What Your Head Is Really Up To* (London: Guardian Books, 2017); Yuval Noah Harari, *Sapiens: A Brief History of Human Kind* (New York: Harper Collins, Publishers, 2015); and Cailin O'Conner and James Owen Weatherall, *The Misinformation Age: How False Beliefs Spread* (New Haven, CT: Yale University Press, 2019). See also their podcast "How Science Spreads: Smallpox, Stomach Ulcers and the Vegetable Lamb of Tartary," NPR Hidden Brain Podcast, January 21, 2019, http://www.npr.org2019/01/11; Michael Shermer, *Why People Believe Weird Things: Pseudoscience, Superstitions and Other Confusions of Our Time* (New York: W.H. Freeman, 1997); and Michael Shermer, *The Believing Brain: From Ghosts and Gods to Politics and Conspiracies* (St. Petersburg, FL: Time Publishing, 2011).

58. John Brockman, ed., *What We Believe but Cannot Prove: Today's Leading Thinkers on Science in the Age of Certainty* (New York: Harper Perennial, 2006), XI.

59. Ibid., 251.

60. Cohen, *Encyclopedia of Ghosts*, 163–67; Daniel R. Jennings, *The Supernatural Occurrences of John Wesley (*Oklahoma City: Sean Multimedia, 2005); Stephen Tompkins, *John Wesley: A Biography* (Grand Rapids, MI: William B. Eerdmans, 2003).

61. Gladys Barr, *The Bell Witch of Adams* (Nashville, TN: David Hutchison, 1969); and *The Ghost at Epworth Rectory: A Tale of the Wesley Ghost* (Nashville, TN: David Hutchison, 1970).

62. William Nabors, "True Ghost Stories, Part I," *Guntersville Advertise-Gleam*, February 7, 1940; and Floy Beatty, "Bell Witch Broke Her Date," *Nashville Tennessean*, April 9, 1972.

63. Edwards, *Ghostly Whispers*, 94.

64. "Christians Can Believe in the Bell Witch," *Nashville Tennessean*, October 31, 2006.

65. Bruce M. Metzger and Michael D. Cougan, eds., *The Oxford Companion to the Bible* (New York: Oxford University Press, 1993).

66. "Likes Book Page," *Nashville Banner*, July 10, 1961.

67. James W. Loewen, *Lies My Teacher Told Me: Everything Your American History Textbook Got Wrong* (New York: The New Press, 1990), 1; and Mark A Stoler, *A Skeptic's Guide to American History* (Chantilly, VA: The Teaching Company, 2012), audio CD.

68. Phillip Deloria, "The Invention of Thanksgiving: Massacres, Myths, and the making of the Great November Holiday," *New Yorker*, November 25, 2019, 70–74.

69. Jeff Jordan, *Pascal's Wager: Pragmatic Arguments and Belief in God* (London: Oxford University Press, 2007).

70. Schermer, *Why People Believe Weird Things: Pseudoscience, Superstition, and Other Confusions of Our Time* (New York: Macmillan, 1997), 46–61.

71. Neil Dagnall and Dr. Ken Drinkwater, "The Science of Superstition- and Why People Believe," Manchester Metropolitan University, July 2, 2018, https://www.mmu.ac.uk/news-and-events/news/story/?id=80811 (article removed).

72. George V. Triplett, "The Strange Survival of the Demon Idea," *Louisville Courier-Journal*, March 27, 1898; *Iowa Press-Citizen*, October 31, 1983. See *St. Cloud Times* (MN), October 28, 1983; and *Sioux Falls* (SD) *Argos-Leader*, November 13, 1983, for more examples of the "mirror story."

73. Ellie Haskin and Jesse Fivecoate, *Encounters Episode 18: The One About the Bell Witch* (feat. Brandon Barker), May 25, 2017, in encounterscast.com.

74. Ibid.

75. "Marshall Library Gets Tough to Reclaim Missing Materials," November 25, 2004. See also, "Spirited Away, BW Books Return," *Nashville Banner*, May 8, 1956.

76. Dr. Christopher Dwyer, "5 Reasons We Enjoy Being Scared," *Psychology Today*, October 19, 2018, psychologytoday.com. See also, Burnett, *Idiot Brain*, 96–100.

77. O'Conner and Weatherall, *Misinformation Age*, 16–17.

78. Ibid.

79. Harari, *Sapiens*, 180.

80. "What Others Say," *Johnson City Press*, April 16, 1937.

81. William Safire, "On Language Suspension of Disbelief," *New York Times*, October 7, 2007; and Norman Holland, "Spiderman? Sure! The Neuroscience of Disbelief," *Interdisciplinary Science Reviews*, December 2008, 312–20.

Chapter 2

1. As I write this story, I will focus on four of the earliest and best-known renditions of the legend. The first is M. V. Ingram, *An Authenticated History of the Famous Bell Witch. The Wonder of the 19th Century, and Unexplained Phenomenon of the Christian Era* (Clarksville, TN: W.P. Titus Press, 1894; Nashville, TN: Rare Books Reprints, 1961). Supposedly, John Bell's son Richard Williams Bell wrote a piece in his journal entitled "Our Family Trouble" in 1846 and passed it to his son, Allen Bell. Ingram included "Our Family Trouble" in his *Authenticated History*. The journal has never been found. In 1934, another descendant of John and Lucy Bell, Charles Baily Bell, wrote *A Mysterious Spirit: The Bell Witch of Tennessee, which* was also reprinted in 1972 by Charles Elder in Nashville. Harriet Parks Miller, a resident of Adams, Tennessee, wrote *The Bell Witch of Middle Tennessee* in 1930, which was printed by the *Clarksville Leaf-Chronicle Publishing Co.* and was reprinted with the Charles Bailey Bell book in 1934.

2. William Gay, "Queen of the Haunted Dell," *Oxford American*, September/October 2000, 54–62. For readers who want more information about why people believe what they cannot prove and why there are variations of well-known stories, see the study by Tom Peete Cross cited in chapter one. Also see Carl Sagan, *The Demon-Haunted World: Science as a Candle in the Dark* (New York: Ballantine Books, 1996); and Peter Aykroyd, *A History of Ghosts: The True Story of Seances, Mediums, Ghosts, and Ghostbusters* (Emmaus, PA: Rodale Books, 2009).

3. Timothy R. Henson, *The Black Patch Bells: The Story of John and Lucy Bell* (self-published, 2003), 2–3, 63.

4. Gay, "Queen of the Haunted Dell," 61–62.

5. Dickson D. Bruce Jr., *And they all Sang Hallelujah: Plain-Folk Camp-Meeting Religion, 1800-1845* (Knoxville: University of Tennessee Press, 1974); John B. Boles, *The Great Revival, 1787–1805: Origins of the Southern Evangelical Mind* (Lexington: University of Kentucky Press, 1972); Herman A. Norton, *Religion in Tennessee, 1777–1945* (Knoxville: University of Tennessee Press, 1981); Edward

Coffman, *The Story of Logan County* (Nashville, TN: Parthenon Press, 1962), 74–88.

6. The Red River Meeting House was approximately twenty miles to the front door of the Bell House at Red River, now Adams.

7. Boles, *Great Revival*, 67–68; Norton, *Religion in Tennessee*, 23–26; and Reuben Ross, *Life and Times of Elder Reuben Ross*, ed. James Ross (Nashville: McQuiddy Printing, 1977).

8. Norton, *Religion in Tennessee*, 23–25.

9. Paul Conkin, *Cane Ridge: America's Pentecost* (Madison: University of Wisconsin Press, 1976), 108.

10. Ibid, 99–100.

11. Peter Cartwright, *Autobiography of Peter Cartwright*, centennial ed. (Nashville, TN: Abingdon Press, 1956), 43–49.

12. Reuben Ross, *Life and Times*, 20.

13. Ibid, 21, 30–31.

14. Anita Wadhwani, "Christians Can Believe in Bell Witch, Town Says," *Nashville Tennessean*, October 31, 2006.

15. John J. Collins, ed. *The Oxford Handbook of Apocalyptic Literature* (Oxford: Oxford University Press, 2014); Mark O'Connell, *Notes From an Apocalypse: A Personal Journey to the End of the World and Back* (New York: Doubleday, 2020).

16. Robert Burnham and David H. Levy, *Great Comets* (New York: Cambridge University Press, 2000), 53; Patrick Moore, *The Data Book of Astronomy* (Philadelphia: CRC Press, 2013), 233.

17. Leo Tolstoy, *War and Peace* (Garden City, NY: International Collectors' Library, 1949), 363, reprint.

18. Jay Feldman, *When the Mississippi Ran Backwards: Empire, Intrigue, Murder, and the New Madrid Earthquakes* (New York: Free Press, 2005), 232–35.

19. Ibid, 234.

20. Cartwright, *Autobiography*, 30.

21. Ibid., 126.

22. Ross, *Life and Times*, 201–05.

23. Ibid, 198–99.

24. Jason C. Bivins, *Thinking about Religion and Violence: Course Guidebook* (Chantilly, VA: The Teaching Company, 2018), 46.

Chapter 3

1. Tamin Ansary, *The Invention of Yesterday: A 30,000 Year History of Human Culture, Conflict, and Connection* (New York: Public Affairs, 2019).

2. Richard Russo "The Lives of Others: When Imagination Became Appropriation," *Harper's Magazine,* June 2020, 27.

3. Tim O' Brien, *The Things They Carried* (Boston: Mariner Books, 2009), 27.

4. Tristram Coffin, "Mary Hamilton and the Anglo-American Ballad as an Art Form," *Journal of American Folklore,* 70 (1957), 208–14. See also, Meg Bowles, et al., *How to Tell a Story* (New York: Crown, 2022).

5. "Core Emotions," uwv.edu. See also, Anne Hawly, "Discover Your Stories," curestorygrid.com; and David Leeming, *Storytelling Encyclopedia: Historical, Cultural, and Multiethnic Approaches to Oral Traditions Around the World* (Westport CT: Breenwood, 1997).

6. B. A. Botkin, *A Treasury of Southern Folklore: Stories, Ballads, Traditions, and Folkways of the People of the South* (New York: Corwin Publishers, 1949), 470.

7. Emma B. Miles, *The Spirit of the Mountains* (New York: James Pott, 1905), 108–17.

8. For an academic explanation of the various versions of the mirror story, see K. Brandon Barker and Claiborne Rice, *Folk Illusions: Children, Folklore, and Sciences of Perception* (Bloomington: Indiana University Press, 2019), 136–60, 205–06.

9. For another academic explanation see, Alan Dundes, "Bloody Mary in the Mirror: A Ritual Reflection of Pre-pubescent Anxiety," *Western Folklore,* 57 (1998): 119–35.

10. *Candyman,* Robert Ebert, film review, Rogerebert.com.

11. Henson, *Black Patch Bells,* 58–68; and Edwards, *Something Wicked* (Self-published, 2019), 113–16.

12. Donald Davidson, ed., *The Critics Almanac: Another South. Knoxville Journal,* December 9, 1928, 36.

13. Arthur Palmer Hudson, *Specimens of Mississippi Folklore* (Ann Arbor MI: Edwards Brothers, 1928).

14. Davidson, *Critics Almanac,* 36. See also, Alan Brown, "The Grave of Elizabeth 'Betsy' Bell," *Mississippi Legends and Lore* (Mount Pleasant, SC: the History Press, 2000).

15. Arthur Palmer Hudson and Pete Kyle McCarter, *The Journal of American Folklore,* 47, no. 183 (Jan-Mar 1934): 45–63.

16. Findagrave.com

17. Jonah Craig, "The Bell Witch from an American Legend," *Playboy,* November, 1968, 149; "Return of the Bell Witch," in Nancy Roberts, *Ghosts of the Southern Mountains and Appalachia* (Columbia: University of South Carolina Press, 2019), 8–16; and Pat Fitzhugh, "The Bell Witch of North Carolina," http://www.bellwitch.org.

18. M. V. Ingram, *An Authenticated History of the Famous Bell Witch. The Wonder of the 19th Century, and Unexplained Phenomenon of the Christian Era* (Clarksville, TN: W.P. Titus Press, 1894; Nashville, TN: Rare Books Reprints, 1961), 7.

19. Ibid., 238–307.

20. Ibid., 101–88.

21. Miller, *The Bell Witch of Tennessee* (Clarksville: Leaf-Chronicle Publishing Co., 1930), reprinted with the Charles Bailey Bell, *Bell Witch of Tennessee*, 1934. The book was later republished in 1934 in conjunction with Charles Bailey Bell's book, *The Bell Witch of Tennessee*, p. 246.

22. Bell, *Bell Witch*, 7.

23. Ibid., 8.

24. *Nashville Tennessean*, October 1, 1937.

25. John F. Baker Jr., *The Washington's of Wessyngton Plantation: Stories of My Family's Journey to Freedom* (New York: Atria Books, 2009), 144.

26. Ingram, *Authenticated History*, 219–28; Richard Williams Bell, "Our Family Trouble," *Authenticated History*, 35–37; Miller, *Bell Witch*, 49–50.

27. There will be a more complete discussion of this program in Chapter 4.

28. Joseph Petrocelli, *Folklore and Folklife Collection* (Chicago: University of Chicago Press, 1970), 42.

29. Josephine Lombardo, *Bell Witch Legends*, Bloomington, Indiana University Archives of Traditional Music, 1972, 8 sound cassettes and documentation.

30. Josephine Lombardo interview with Ralph Winters, June 6, 1972.

31. Middle Tennessee State University, September 30, 2017.

Chapter 4

1. "Oldest Guthrie Citizen," *Nashville Tennessean*, August 4, 1899.

2. "From Letters to the American," *Nashville American*, July 7, 1910.

3. Jim Brooks, *Bell Witch Stories You Never Heard, From the Family That Lived Next Door* (Princeton, KY: McClanahan, 2015), 196–203; Pat Fitzhugh, *The Bell Witch, The Full Account* (Nashville, TN: Armand, 2000), 292–323.

4. Gillen Wood, *Tambora: The Eruption that Changed the World* (Princeton, NJ: Princeton University Press, 2014).

5. Bret E. Carroll, *Spiritualism in Antebellum America* (Bloomington: Indiana University Press, 1997).

6. "Can Psychics Speak to the Dead?," *The Week*, April 15, 2019, 36–37.

7. Charles Edwin Price, *The Infamous Bell Witch of Tennessee* (Johnson City, TN: Overmountain Press, 1994), 82–83.

8. Jess Stearn, *The Sleeping Prophet* (New York: Bantam Books, 1967).

9. "The Tennessee Ghost," *New England Farmer,* January 26, 1856; "The Tennessee Ghost," *The New England Farmer,* February 7, 1856. See also, Pat Fitzhugh, *The Bell Witch: The Full Account* (Nashville: Armand Press, 2009), 171–72.

10. Dewey Edwards, *Execution of Murder: Robertson County, Tennessee Murder Cases, 1810–1910* (Self-published, 2005), 28–29.

11. "Witchcraft and Murder, Hobgoblins and Old Gray Horses the Incentive to Crime," *Louisville Courier-Journal,* September 21, 1868. See also, "Clinard-Burgess," *Nashville Union and American,* March 20, 1869. In *The Authenticated History of the Bell Witch,* Mrs. Lucinda E. Rawls informed Ingram of the link between the Bell Witch and the Clinard-Burgess murder, 250–51.

12. "A Real Ghost Story: Springfield Terribly Excited Over Mysterious Manifestations," *Nashville Daily American,* April 27, 1880; "Springfield's Ghost," *Nashville Daily American,* April 28, 1880; "The Springfield Spook Sensation," *Nashville Daily American,* April 30, 1880. For a retrospective view of the story see Deborah Highland, "Local Legends and Halloween Lore," *Nashville Tennessean,* October 30, 1996.

13. *The Goodspeed Histories of Montgomery, Robertson, Humphreys, Steward, Dickson, Cheatham, Houston Counties of Tennessee* (Columbia, TN: Woodward & Stinson, 1972; reprint), 833. See also Fred S. Rolater, "Goodspeed Histories," in Carroll Van West, ed., *The Tennessee Encyclopedia of History and Culture* (Nashville, TN: Rutledge Hill, 1998), 370.

14. *Goodspeed Histories,* 833.

15. Charles H. Love, *Springfield's First 100 Years* (Springfield TN: Robertson County Historical Society, 2003, reprint) 29; W. P. Titus, *Picturesque Clarksville: Past and Present* (Clarksville, TN: 1973 reprint).

16. The article was entitled "An Interesting Book." For more information concerning Ingram and the *Leaf-Chronicle,* see Jack Cook, "The Spirit of Red River," bellwitchmts.blogspot.com.

17. A. S. Mott, *Ghost Stories of Tennessee* (Auburn, WA: Lone Pine, 2005), 7.

18. Ingram, *Authenticated History,* 229–33.

19. Seth Godin, *Purple Cow: Transform Your Business by Being Remarkable* (New York: Portfolio, 2003).

20. "Andrew Jackson and the Bell Witch," POTUS7 Podcast, https://thehermitage.com/andrew-jackson-and-the-bell-witch/.

Chapter 5

1. See *Chattanooga Daily Times,* August 2, 1907; *Knoxville Sentinel,* October 6, 1909.

2. *Clarksville Leaf-Chronicle*, November 26, 1918, November 26, 1918, January 23, 1930, June 11, 1941, August 23, 1941, August 26, 1941.

3. *Nashville Tennessean*, May 21, 1961, April 9, 1961.

4. *Clarksville Leaf-Chronicle*, December 23, 1964, July 21, 1968, November 5, 1969.

5. *Hopkinsville Kentuckian*, March 12, 1895.

6. *Clarksville Tobacco-Leaf Chronicle*, December 7, 1900.

7. W. L. Duggan, "Sketches of Sevier and Robertson Counties," *The American Historical Magazine*, June 1900, 310–25.

8. "The Bell Witch Up Again," *Clarksville Leaf-Chronicle*, August 14, 1903.

9. *Hopkinsville Kentuckian*, September 15, 1903. During this period, the *Springfield Herald's* office burned, thus, we have no articles directly from it.

10. For examples, see *Nashville Banner*, January 16, 1916; *Chattanooga News*, July 5, 1924, May 9, 1925; *Clarksville Leaf-Chronicle*, March 8, 1922.

11. Irvin S. Cobb, "A Witch as Was a Witch," *McClure's Magazine*, March 1922, 18–21; *Chattanooga Times*, May 17, 1925.

12. Harriet Miller, *The Bell Witch of Middle Tennessee* (Clarksville: *Clarksville Leaf-Chronicle*, 1930). For a review see, *Nashville Banner*, February 22, 1931.

13. See *Knoxville Journal*, May 11, 1930, March 6, 1932; Mary Lanier Magruder, "Regarding Things Old and New," *Paducah Sun Democrat*, October 30, 1932; Martha Barnett, "Beware Tennessee's Bell Witch," *Chattanooga Daily Times*, March 26, 1933.

14. T. H. Alexander, "I Reckon So," *Nashville Tennessean*, October 15, 1932.

15. *Des Moines Register*, September 29, 1935. See also, M. B. Morton, "Dire Prediction of the Bell Witch," *Nashville Banner*, August 11, 1935.

16. *Nashville Tennessean*, January 3, 1937. See also, https://tennesseehistory .org/year-of-the-witch/.

17. James R. Aswell, et al., *God Bless the Devil! Liars' Bench Tales* (Chapel Hill: University of North Carolina Press, 1940).

18. *Memphis Commercial Appeal*, January 11, 1948.

19. Bill Holder, "The Rowdy Witch," *Nashville Tennessean Magazine*, March 21, 1948.

20. Hans Holzer, "Glamour Queens and ESP," September 17, 1967.

21. *Lincoln Journal Star*, December 3, 1967.

22. Andrew Tackaberry, *Famous Ghosts, Phantoms, Poltergeists for the Millions* (New York: Bell Publishing, 1967), 79–91; Peggy Robbins, "Kate, The Bell Witch," *Exploring the Unknown*, March 1968, 21–33.

23. Hugh Walker, "Here Comes Kate!," *Nashville Tennessean*, April 2, 1972.

24. Christopher Dafoe, "The Causerie," *Vancouver Sun*, February 9, 1973.

25. "Tales of Eerie Haunts and Apparitions," *Wisconsin Rapids Daily Tribune*, October 25, 1986.

26. Susy Smith, *Ghosts Around the House* (New York: World Publishing, 1970), 165–69; Mary Bolte, *Dark and Bloodied Ground: Devilish Tales from Virginia, West Virginia, North Carolina, Tennessee, and Kentucky*, (New York: Hawthorne Books, 1973), 27-28; J. T. Gouch, The Pennyrile, Michael Andrew Grissom, *Southern by the Grace of God* (Gretna, LA: Pelican Publishing, 1999), 380–87; Natalie Osborne-Thomason, *The Ghost-Hunting Casebook* (London, UK: Bland-ford, 1999), 183.

27. *Sacramento Bee*, November 1, 2003

28. *Vancouver Sun*, October 30, 2004.

29. *Danville Advocate-Messenger*, October 25, 2009.

30. *Anniston* (AL) *Star*, June 19, 2011.

31. *Nashville Tennessean*, June 14, 2006.

32. Mark Mihalko, "Bell's Hell, Tennessee's Bell Witch Continues to Haunt Audiences on Screen and Off," *Haunted Times Magazine*, Fall 2005, 20; Brad Steiger, "The Ghost of Old Kate Batts, the Bell Witch," in *Real Ghosts, Restless Spirits and Haunted Places* (Detroit, MI: Detroit Visible Ink Press, 2012), 91–98; Mott, "The Bell Witch," *Ghost Stories of Tennessee*, 123–44.

Chapter 6

1. *Knoxville: University of Tennessee Press*, 1982.

2. *Journal of American Folklore*, 22, 1909, 253.

3. *Journal of American Folklore*, Jan–Mar, 1934, 4563.

4. *Chapel Hill* (NC) *Daily Tar Hill*, "Hudson Will Speak on the Legend of Old South," February 5, 1933; "Five Faculty to Read Papers at Meeting Soon," November 18, 1932; "A.P. Hudson Spreads Story to North Carolina," November 29, 1932.

5. "The Bell Witch: An Overseeing Haunt," in Jane Polley, ed., *American Folklore and Legend: The Saga of our Heroes and Heroines, Our Braggers, Boosters and Mad Men, Our Beliefs and Superstitions* (Pleasantville, NY: *Reader's Digest*, 1978), 134–35.

6. Harry A. Hargrave, "Demonic Visits of the Bell Witch," *North Carolina Folklore Journal*, May 1975, 47–55. For other folklore articles, see James T. Pearce, "Folklore Tales of the Southern Poor-White, 1820-1860," *Journal of American Folklore*, October–December 1950, 398–412; "The Famous Bell Witch," *Tennessee Conservationist*, June 1959, 11, 21; Jack Welsh, "The Bell Witch," *Kentucky Folklore Record*, October–December 1973, 112–16; Gladys Barr,

"Witchcraft in Tennessee," *Tennessee Valley Historical Review,* Fall 1973, 24–29; Teresa A. Lockhart, "20th Century Aspects of the Bell Witch," *Tennessee Folklore Society Bulletin,* 50 (1984): 18–24; and William Gay, "Queen of the Haunted Dell," *Oxford American,* September/October 2000, 54–62.

7. *Nashville Banner,* December 16, 1934.

8. *Nashville Tennessean,* January 19, 1947.

9. "Ghost Course Not Scaring Off TTU Students: Popular Class Looks at History Behind Legends," *The Nashville Tennessean,* October 13, 2006.

10. *Nashville Tennessean,* August 6, 2011.

11. *The Oxford Daily Mississippian,* October 31, 2017.

12. Michael Owen Jones, ed., *Putting Folklore to Use* (Lexington: University Press of Kentucky, 1994), 9, 11.

13. Stith Thompson, *Motif-Index of Folk-Literature,* 6 vols. (Bloomington: Indiana University Press, 1960); Ernest W. Baughman, *Type and Motif Index of the Folktales of England and North America* (The Hauge: Mouton, 1966, Indiana University Folklore Series No. 20).

14. For other motif studies, see Kathy Johnson, "The Legend of the Bell Witch," *North Carolina Folklore Journal,* August 1976, 43–48; Charles Edwin Price, *Haints, Witches and Boogers: Tales from Upper East Tennessee* (Winston-Salem, NC: John F. Blair, 1992).

15. Bill Ellis, *Lucifer Ascending: The Occult in Folklore and Popular Culture* (Lexington: University of Kentucky Press, 2004).

16. Alan Schwartz, "The Big Toe," in *Scary Stories to Tell in the Dark* (New York: Harper & Row, 1981), 7–9.

17. Hereward Carrington and Nandor Fodor, *Haunted People: Story of the Poltergeist Down the Centuries* (New York: E.P. Dutton, 1951); Nandor Fodor, "Psychoanalyzing the Bell Witch," *FATE,* September 1952, 85–109; Nandor Fodor, *On the Trail of the Poltergeist* (New York: Citadel Press, 1958); Nandor Fodor, *The Haunted Mind: A Psychoanalyst Looks at the Supernatural* (New York: Garrett, 1959).

18. Robert Somerlott, Here Mr. Splitfoot: An Informal Exploration into Modern Occultism (New York: Viking Press, 1971).

19. New York: Harper Collins, 1994.

20. Brent Monahan, *The Bell Witch: An American Haunting* (New York: St. Martin's Griffin, 1997); *An American Haunting,* directed by Courtney Solomon (Lionsgate,2005).

21. Pat Fitzhugh, *The Bell Witch: The Full Account* (Nashville, TN: Armand, 2000).

22. *Chattanooga Daily Times,* November 20, 1949.

23. Jonah Craig, "The Bell Witch: From an American Legend," *Playboy Magazine*, November 1968, 149.

24. Patti Carr Black, "Let's Start Talking Again," *Clarke County Tribune*, March 20, 1986.

25. Pam Cassady, "Logan County Stories of Strange Happenings," *Russellville News Democrat* (KY) *and Leader*

26. Bill Rollow, "This is my Story," *Montgomery Advertiser*, July 25, 1939.

27. Urith Lucas, "Stories of Illinois 'Angelic Spirit' Revives Memories of Robertson County's Mysterious Bell Witch Activities," *Nashville Banner*, October 1, 1949.

28. "Big Ghost Scare Recalls Bell Witch," *Nashville Banner*, March 12, 1922.

29. Works Progress Writers' Project, *Tennessee: A Guide to the State* (New York: Viking Press, 1939).

30. *Nashville Tennessean*, March 9, 1986.

31. *Murfreesboro Daily News-Journal*, October 22, 1999, September 2, 2018; *Nashville Tennessean*, September 30, 2005, September 6, 2015.

32. *Ashland City Times*, October 16, 2019.

33. Carroll Van West, ed. *The Tennessee Encyclopedia of History and Culture* (Nashville: Tennessee Historical Society and Rutledge Press, 1998), 59–60.

Chapter 7

1. Melissa Sanders-Self, *All that Lives, A Novel of the Bell Witch* (New York: Warner Books, 2002), viii.

2. See also, "Does the Bell Witch Live on?," *Red Bank* (NJ) *Daily Register*, October 31, 1977; "We Together: Fear of the Unknown Often Gives Rise to Superstitions and Weird Beliefs," *Dayton Herald*, August 30, 1938; "Town Bewitched by Local Legend," *Middletown Times Herald* (NY), November, 1, 1976; "Bell Witch Tales Keep Legend Alive in Tennessee Farm Area," *Indianapolis Star*, October 31, 1977.

3. For more information about Eden, see H. C. Brehm, *Echoes of the Bell Witch in the Twentieth Century* (Nashville: Mini Histories, 1984); Robert Dollar, "Bewitched But not Bothered," *Clarksville Leaf-Chronicle*, July 10, 1981; Blake Fontenay, "Bell Witch: Unseeing 's Believing," *Nashville Banner*, October 29, 1986.

4. Articles about Turner's retelling can be found in numerous newspaper articles in Tennessee and Kentucky. An example is "Bell Witch Introduced to Fort Campbell Students," *Clarksville Leaf-Chronicle*, April 22, 1973.

5. Davidson spoke on the "Bell Witch of Tennessee" at the Ridgetop (TN) Storytelling Festival. "Bell Witch View," *Nashville Tennessean*, April 6, 1996. This is just one of numerous times Davidson spoke on the subject.

6. Dewey Edwards, *Something Wicked!: The Bell Witch Phenomenon* (Self-published, 2007); *Ghostly Whispers* (Self-published, 2019); Timothy R. Henson, *The Black Patch Bells* (Self-published, 2003); Pat Fitzhugh, *The Bell Witch: The Full Account* (Nashville, TN: Armand Press, 2009); *The Bell Witch Haunting* (Nashville, TN: Armond, 1999).

7. For examples, see Carmita Hedges, "To Talk of Many Things," *Tahlequah* (OK) *Star Citizen*, October 27, 1960.

8. Examples of the numerous articles about her include Susan Wilson, "Story Lady is a Legend in Her Own Time," *Boston Globe*, February 23, 1984.

9. Patti Carr Black, "Ghoules and Ghosts: Let's Start Talking Again," *Clarke County* (MS) *Tribune*, March 20, 1986. See also "With the Scouts at Camp Boswell," *Nashville Banner*, July 5, 1930; "Bell Witch Dance at Birthday Fete," *Madisonville* (KY) *Messenger*, October 13, 1937; "7th Grade Language Arts Class Gathered to Hear Bell Witch Stories," *Johnson City* (TN) *Press*, October 25, 2006.

10. Carolyn Livingston, *Charles Faulkner Bryan: His Life and Music* (Knoxville: University of Tennessee Press, 2003); "The Bell Witch to Music," *Nashville Tennessean*, April 13, 1947; "The Bell Witch Wins Applause," *Nashville Tennessean*, April 15, 1947.

11. *Pasadena* (CA) *Independent*, May 9, 1954.

12. "Modern Dance," *Nashville Tennessean*, May 14, 1961, May 20, 1961.

13. "A Bewitching Program," *Nashville Tennessean*, October 5, 2001.

14. For examples, see Karin Miller, "Witch Tale Rings a Bell with Tennessee Family," *Tampa Tribune*, October 27, 2003.

15. "Bell Witch Nominated Worldwide," *Nashville Tennessean*, March 7, 2004, October 25, 2008.

16. Nellie McCaslin, *Tall Tales and Tall Men* (Philadelphia, PA: Macrae Smith, 1956).

17. *Boston Globe*, April 28, 1957.

18. *Santa Cruz* (CA) *Sentinel*, May 17, 1959; *Davenport* (IA) *Daily Times*, July 8, 1957; *Richmond Times Dispatch*, August 5, 1956.

19. *Passaic* (NJ) *Herald-News*, December 8, 1966; *Lincoln* (NE) *Journal Star*, April 10, 1977; *Russellville* (KY) *News Democrat*, March 17, 1966; *Clarksville Leaf-Chronicle*, May 26, 1974.

20. "Girls at Buford College Contribute to the Democratic Fund," *Nashville Tennessean*, November 10, 1912.

21. *Nashville Tennessean*, September 29, 1957; *White Plains* (NY), July 19, 1981. *New York Daily News*, July 19, 1981; *Charlotte Observer*, February 5, 1993; *Atlanta Constitution*, October 27, 2002.

22. Much valuable information about this topic can be found in Austin Peay State University's Felix G. Woodward Library, University Archives and Special Collections, The Bell Witch Collection. See also *Memphis Commercial Appeal*, May 17, 1987; *Clarksville Leaf-Chronicle*, October 23, 1986; *Nashville Tennessean*, May 2, 1987.

23. *Nashville Tennessean*, May 31, 1974.

24. *Honolulu Star Bulletin*, October 31, 1976.

25. *Beckley* (WV) *Post Herald*, October 31, 1976; *Honolulu* (HI) *Advertiser*, October 31, 1986; *Twin Falls* (ID) *Times-News*, October 31, 1976; *Kenosha* (WI) *News*, November 2, 1976; *Arizona Republic*, October 31, 1976; *Springfield* (MO) *Leader Press*, October 31, 1976; *Nashville Tennessean*, October 31, 1976.

26. *Nashville Tennessean*, October 18, 1987.

27. *Nashville Tennessean*, October 11, 1998, October 12, 2003, October 16, 2008.

28. Doug Henning with Charles Reynolds *Houdini: His Legend and His Magic* (New York: Times Books, 1978).

29. "The Arts," *Captiva* (WI) *Times*, November 29, 1984.

30. "Master of Double Talk Plays Stooge to a Dummy," *Louisville Courier-Journal*, March 14, 1943.

Chapter 8

1. Jane and Michael Stern, *Encyclopedia of Pop Culture* (New York: Harper Collins, 1992), xi.

2. *USA Today*, January 16, 1996; Jill Lepore, *These Truths: A History of the United States* (New York: W.W. Norton, 2018), 422.

3. *Nashville Tennessean*, May 30, 1937, June 1, 1937. See also, *Nashville Banner*, July 1, 1937.

4. *Richmond Times Dispatch*, September 14, 1941.

5. *Louisville Courier-Journal*, September 14, 1941; *Wisconsin State Journal*, September 14, 1941; *Sacramento* (CA) *Bee*, September 13, 1941; *Sioux City* (IA) *Journal*, September 13, 1941.

6. *St. Louis* (MO) *Post-Dispatch*, April 28, 1946.

7. *Camden* (NJ) *Courier Post*, December 26, 1964; *Wausau* (WI) *Daily Herald*, November 6, 1964.

8. Mercyful Fate lyrics, songs, and albums, https://www.lyricsfreak.com/m/mercyful+fate/; Mercyful Fate, "The Bell Witch," https://www.metal-archives.com/bands/Mercyful_Fate/182.

9. "The Shakers find Plenty of Success Thanks to the Power of the Bell

Witch," *Nashville Tennessean*, September 30, 1988; "The Shakers Bell Witch Music," https://www.last.fm/music/The+Shakers.

10. https://bellwitch.bandcamp.com/; https://www.songkick.com/artists /4737848-bell-witch; *Vancouver Province*, September 24, 2015 and *San Francisco Examiner*, December 5, 2017.

11. *Bellingham* (WA) *Herald*, May 17, 2012.

12. H. P. Lovecraft, *Supernatural Horror in Literature* (1945; New York: Dover, 1973), 12. See also Michael Kelahan, *The Screaming Skull and Other Classic Horror Stories* (New York: Fall River, 2010); James B. Twitchell, *Dreadful Pleasures: An Anatomy of Modern Horror* (Oxford: Oxford University Press, 1985); Bill Ellis, *Lucifer Ascending: The Occult in Folklore and Popular Culture* (Lexington: University Press of Kentucky, 2004).

13. August 2, 1997.

14. Gladys Barr, *The Bell Witch of Adams* (Nashville, TN: David Hutchison, 1969); Sharon Sigmond Shebar and Judith Schoder, *The Bell Witch* (New York: Julian Messner, 1983); Daniel Cohen, *Young Ghosts* (New York: Scholastic, 1994); Jen Jones, *Bone Chilling Ghost Stories* (North Mankato, MN: Capstone, 2014).

15. Waterville, (ME): Thorndike, 2003, 38.

16. David J. Skal, *The Monster Show: A Cultural History of Horror* (New York: Farrar, Straus and Giroux, 1993); Charles Derry, *Dark Dreams: A Psychological History of the Modern Horror Film From the 1950s to the 21st Century* (Jefferson, NC: McFarland, 2009).

17. Derry, 21-22.

18. "Box Office Performance for Horror Movies in 2018," https://the -numbers.com/market/2018/genre/ horror and for 2019, https://www.the -numbers.com/market/2019/genre/horror.

19. Kyle William Bishop, *How Zombies Conquered Popular Culture: They Multifarious Walking Dead in the 21st Century* (Jefferson, NC: McFarland, 2015); Ashley Szanter and Jessica K. Richards (eds.) *Romancing the Zombie: Essays on the Undead as Significant "Other"* (Jefferson, NC: McFarland, 2017).

20. Derry, 22.

21. *Nashville Tennessean*, April 17, 2006; and *Santa Clarita* (CA) *Signal*, November 6, 2013.

22. Lepore, *These Truths*, 557–67.

23. "LSTC English Department has TV Program," *Our Southern Home*, (Livingston, AL), May 12, 1955; and *Nashville Tennessean*, March 5, 1975.

24. *Abbotsford* (BC) *News*, October 24, 2000; *Oklahoma City Daily Oklahoman*, October 26, 2000; *Kenosha* (WI) *News*, October 27, 2000; Edmonton (Alberta), September 20, 2002.

25. *Nashville Tennessean,* October 20, 2005; *Franklin* (KY) *Favorite,* May 18, 2006.

26. http://www.ket.org/series/KBEL.

27. Just a few examples are *Ottawa* (Canada) *Citizen,* October 30, 2015; *Honolulu Star-Advertiser,* November 8, 2015; *Fort Collins Coloradan,* October 26, 2015; *Hackensack* (NJ) *Record,* November 22, 2105.

28. *Chippewa* (WI) *Herald-Telegram,* April 6, 2019; *Hackensack Record,* November 18, 2018.

29. Lepore, *These Truths,* 731–33.

30. October 30, 1999. See also, *Nashville Tennessean, October 12, 2003.*

31. https://www.beeradvocate.com/beer/profile/41739/.

32. *Boston Globe,* October 29, 1991; *Hartford* (CT) *Courant,* November 7, 1991; *New York Daily News,* September 18, 1993.

33. Shopnaturetrails.com.

Chapter 9

1. *Clarksville Leaf-Chronicle,* May 5, 2006. See also, "Know Tennessee's Counties: Robertson County is Famous in the Supernatural Realm," *Johnson City Press,* May 21, 1959.

2. Sarah Bartlett, National Geographic Guide to the World's Supernatural Places (Washington, DC: *National Geographic,* 2014), 34. See also Mark Moran and Mark Sceurman, *Weird U.S.: Your Travel Guide to America's Local Legends and Best Kept Secrets* (New York: Sterling Publishing Company, 2009); Tim O'Brien, *Tennessee: Off the Beaten Path: A Guide to Unique Places* (Old Saybrook, CT: Globe Pequot, 1999).

3. Elke Dettmer, "Moving Toward Responsible Tourism: A Role for Folklore," in Michael Owen Jones, ed. *Putting Folklore to Use* (Lexington: University of Kentucky, 1994), 187–97.

4. "Robertson County is the Place to be in October," *Robertson County Times,* October 13, 2010.

5. John Maines, "Thar's Gold in Them Thar Witch's Chills," *Jackson* (MS) *Clarion-Ledger,* October 27, 1987. See also, Ken Beck, "Adams Embraces Spooky History of the Bell Witch," *Nashville Tennessean,* October 14, 2007.

6. "Weird Witch Tales told by Adams Residents," *Clarksville Leaf-Chronicle,* August 6, 1937.

7. *The Daily Oklahoman,* May 14, 2006.

8. A.L. Dorsey letter to W.E. Youree, January 6, 1939. Bell Witch File, History/Genealogy Room, Stokes Brown Public Library, Springfield, Tennessee.

9. "Tennessee Digs Up its Roots," *New York Daily News*, May 4, 1986; "Open Horse Show to be Held August 15 by Bell Witch Club, *Kentucky Enterprise*, July 16, 1970; "Bell Witch Basketball Classic," *Nashville Tennessean*, December 16, 1976; "The Bell Witch Open," https://www.pdga.com/tour/event/36042; "The Bell Witch Café Reborn," *Robertson County Times*, May 9, 2012. J. Rufus Fears, *Life Lessons from the Great Myths*, Course Guidebook (Chantilly VA: The Teaching Company, 2011).

10. *Clarksville Leaf-Chronicle*, August 3, 1935; *Nashville Tennessean*, September 8, 1935; *Clarksville Leaf-Chronicle*, May 22, 1937; *Nashville Tennessean*, August 14, 1937; *Clarksville Leaf-Chronicle*, May 22, 1937, October 21, 1938; *Russellville* (KY) *News Democrat*, July 13, 1939.

11. "Sinister Cave Recalls Tale," *Nashville Tennessean*, November 1, 1959; "Tennessee's Witches, Ghosts Still on the Prowl," *Lansing State Journal*, October 28, 1984; Rosalle Longo, "Old Cave Affected by Batts, Kate Batts," October 25, 1987; "Bell Witch Spirit Captivates Tourists," *Clarksville Leaf-Chronicle*, July 29, 2003; "Hometown Tourist: Beware of The Bell Witch in Adams, Tennessee, Tennessee's Bell Witch Cave Among Ghost Stories on the Web," *Clarksville Leaf-Chronicle*, October 31, 1999; "Travel Channel: Ghost Adventures, Bell Witch Cave," *Tallahassee Democrat*, January 4, 2015; "Red River Canoe," https://www.canoetheredriver.com/.

12. Bell Witch Cave- National Park Service, http://www.gov/nr/publications/sample_nominations/bellwitchcave.pdf.

13. *Hawaii Tribune-Herald*, May 18, 2008; *Petersburg* (VA) *Progress-Index*, May 18, 2008; and *Hartford* (CT) *Courant*, May 18, 2008, serve as examples.

14. Thomas C. Barr, Jr., *Caves of Tennessee, Bulletin 64* (Nashville: State of Tennessee, Department of Conservation and Commerce, Division of Geology, 1961), 394–96.

15. "Does the Bell Witch Still Haunt Adams?" *Brownsville* (TN) *States-Graphic*, December 23, 1977; *Franklin* (TN) *Review Appeal*, October 12, 1986. See also, mentalfloss.com/article/128281/bell-witch-tennessee.

16. "Review of Bruce and Nancy Roberts, *America's Most Haunted Places*," *Charlotte* (NC) *Observer*, April 4, 1976.

17. "Witch Forces Man to Sell Out," *Jackson* (TN) *Sun*, March 2, 1980; "William Eden Services Today in Springfield," *Nashville Tennessean*, October 23, 1988.

18. "Go Spelunking at Bell Witch Cave, Adams," *Nashville Tennessean*, August 12, 2001; Headley, The Truth Exposed.

19. Jane Sale, *Memories of an Era* (Self-published); *Madisonville* (KY) *Messenger*, July 12, 1971.

20. "Thresher's Set Turner's Tale," *Nashville Banner,* July 14, 1993; "Show Features Antique Farm Equipment and Bell Witch Tales," *Nashville Banner,* July 16, 1986.

21. https://www.fairsandfestivals.net/events/details/bell-witch-old-time -and-bluegrass-festival1; "2-Day 'Bell Witch' Bluegrass Festival Gets Started Today," *Nashville Tennessean,* August 17, 1979.

22. "Bell Witch Old-Time Fiddlers Contest at Bell Witch Village, Adams," *Clarksville Leaf-Chronicle,* August 6, 1982.

23. Toni Dew, "Bell Witch Opry, Part of Couple's Dream," *Nashville Banner,* February 11, 1987.

24. Maude Gold-Kiger, *The Treasure Hunter's Guide to Historic Middle Tennessee and South Central Kentucky, Antiques, Flea Markets and Junk Stores* (Nashville: Gold-Kiger, 1993), 66–67; Fronda Throckmorton, *Country Roads of Tennessee* (Castine, MA: Country Roads, 1994).

25. "BW Opry Founder Kenneth Seeley Dead at 60," *Nashville Tennessean,* May 24, 1986; Charlie Appleton, "Adams to Hear Bell Witch Park Plans," *Nashville Banner,* June 19, 1985; Price, *Infamous Bell Witch of Tennessee,* 86.

26. "Bell Witch Opry Goes to Springfield," *Nashville Tennessean,* October 12, 1983; *St. Cloud* (MN) *Times,* January 21, 1985, "Bell Witch Opry Beginning Third Year," *Clarksville Leaf-Chronicle,* March 25, 1983.

27. Freda Herndon, "Bell Witch Opry Taped for Norway, *Nashville Tennessean,* May 30, 1984; Tammy Rankin, "Bell Witch Opry Rings True to Visitors," *Nashville Banner,* May 30, 1984.

28. Renee Vaughn, "Adams Mayor: Bell Witch Park Means Change," *Nashville Tennessean,* June 26, 1985; "Mystery City to Turn Adams into Major Entertainment Site," *Clarksville Leaf-Chronicle,* August 24, 1985.

29. *Salem* (OR) *Statesman Journal,* May 25, 1986; *Richmond* (IN) *Palladium-Item,* May 25, 1986; *Johnson City* (TN) *Press,* February 5, 2003; *Jackson* (TN) *Sun,* February 2, 2003.

30. This information was derived from a pamphlet distributed before and during the event. The pamphlet is in my possession.

31. www.gatewayghosts.com.

32. http://www.bellwitchfallfestival.com/smoke-2016-1.

33. *Nashville Tennessean,* October 13, 2002; "Adams Museum Gets Boost from Bell Witch," December 25, 2002.

34. "A Lip-Smacking Story," *Nashville Tennessean,* October 13, 2002.

35. *Nashville Tennessean,* December 29, 2002; Karin Miller, "Witch Tale Rings a Bell with Tennessee Family," *Tampa Tribune,* October 27, 2003.

36. *Nashville Tennessean,* October 22, 2005, October 12, 2005.

37. "Start a New Tradition with Local Folklore," November 16, 2008.

Epilogue

1. *The Tennessee Magazine,* January 2021, 12.
2. Taff, *The Bell Witch,* 321–22.
3. A. S. Mott, *Ghost Stories of Tennessee,* 144.